LO

LIKE I'V

BEEN

HOW TO HEAL F

VE

NEVE

HURT

OM HEARTBREA

LOVE LIKE I'VE NEVER BEEN HURT

HOW TO HEAL FROM HEARTBREAK

Arionne's copy!!!

Thank you so much for your support!

To my my Lexi! I love you! thanks for taking care of me!

ARIONNE YVETTE WILLIAMS

CONTENTS

LOVE LIKE I'VE NEVER BEEN HURT:
HOW TO HEAL FROM HEARTBREAK.

 For information, address Arionne Yvette, LLC, P.O. Box 3023, Independence, MO 64055.

www.ArionneYvette.com

This is a work of non-fiction. Some names have been changed to conceal the identities of those characterized in this book.

Cover design by Jodi Ann Brewer

www.JodiAnnBrewer.com

To my baby cuzzos (#cousincrew), my youth,
and anybody who has ever suffered a heartbreak,

I wrote these words for you.

INTRODUCTION HAPPILY EVER AFTER

Growing up in the '80's and '90's, I loved to watch Disney animated classics. Disney's Cinderella is my favorite of all time, with Aladdin as a close second. I'm not sure if it was the friendly birds, the singing mice, or Cinderella's kindness that won me over as a little girl, but I loved every minute of the classic tale—the glass slipper, the melting pumpkin, and the enchanted evening of dancing at the Prince's ball. Cinderella faced her challenges with her evil stepmother and stepsisters with the help of a fairy godmother, won her prince and went off to live with him happily ever after.

I grew up dreaming that I would one day have my own happily ever after. I was in no big rush, but I've always looked forward to finding real love and having a husband and family. In high school, I was fairly popular, but I didn't date much. I was really little, had no breasts or any real noticeable curves. Though I had a lot of friends, I don't think my male counterparts saw me as datable, but all that would change in time.

I had my first real boyfriend at age seventeen. We met at a church convention one night and stayed up talking in the hotel lobby all night long. He lived on the other side of the country, but somehow we managed an exciting teenage long distance love affair with the help of email, yahoo talk, and running up our parents' phone bills. We had a blast in those times, especially during college. There were secret visits by train, a true friendship, and cell phones to sustain us. It was a magical time in our lives. Our relationship lasted for 5 years or so and brought a lot of fun and firsts. Ultimately, though, it was not meant to be. So when that relationship ended around age 22, I cried for two days, took a deep breath and made the adjustment.

After some time I was ready to try love again... and again....and again. Each time I was more hopeful than the last. The story of my twenties reads like a love saga that features a parade of men who apparently just weren't the "one." This saga has towering highs and painful lows and is full of excitement, curiosity, passion, joy and, of course, the overwhelming heaviness of heartache. To be honest, I have been disappointed in love more times than not. I have sometimes felt like the poster child for love unrequited, but somehow each time I manage to pick myself up, dust myself off, and try love again–without bitterness, resentment, or regret.

Though my love story is unique, its twists and turns are not uncommon. I know plenty of women who've been knocked down by love and disappointed time and time again. The hurt they've felt is real because the love they had was strong. What do you do after losing in love?

How do you move on after being let down? How do you heal from heartbreak? Does anyone know? Is there any relief to be found? Is there any way to really move forward after the trauma of a break up when love was supposed to be forever? You know, happily ever after.

I wrote this book to declare that there is life after let downs. There is healing for broken hearts. God does not desire for any of us to be forever weighed down with pain of heartache. There are ways to triumph every time we stumble. There is new strength for moving past our sorrows. There is power and inspiration for new life beyond our painful realities. And if you have been hurt by someone and desire that new life, this book is for you. You may have never realized the way the pains of your past are standing in the way of your bright future, but if you want to know the path to get there, I'm writing for you.

Heartbreak ain't no joke and it's all too familiar to me. I know the pain of trying to sleep with a broken heart–tossing and turning all night long only to rise and have heartache greet me early in the morning. I have felt the lowest of lows after the highest of highs. I've been knocked down by love's abandoning departure. I have felt the pain of rejection and suffered through the lingering lonely nights that remain thereafter. But I also know that there is life–real and happy life–to be lived after all the pain. There is a celebration awaiting us all. There is hope and a great future just around the bend in the road. And I know the way to get there. I wrote these words because I want you to join me there.

I had to learn how to heal from heartache the hard way, but I am happy to share my notes with you. I want you to heal from what hurts you. I want you to laugh again and find the joy in living again. Though your circumstances may seem grim, there is grace for you. This painful chapter in your life will come to an end, if you will it so. Those who hurt you have no power to stop you from healing. Your happily ever after is a real place. I know you are ready to get there because you're already reading this book. And I'm here to help you. I'd be honored to journey with you. Thank you for the privilege.

MY PROMISE TO YOU

I understand that this journey towards healing that you are thinking of embarking upon may be scary, but I hope this book will serve as your companion. You and I may never meet, but I promise to share my story and the lessons I've learned in total honesty. This tale is certainly no tell-all, but it will be transparent. I promise to be honest about my own hurt and honest with you about how I got through it. With that said...Let's go.

Meet me...

I am
#TheBreakUpQueen
#LoveUnrequitedsPosterChild
#NobodysBoo

And at one time I lived in a land called #ILoveYouArionneBut...

Here's my story.

PART I WAITING FOR LOVE

CHAPTER ONE | LOVE YOU ARIONNE BUT..

"I dig you. I think you're pretty. I think you're smart. I like your spirit, your attitude. I like the way you carry yourself. I damn near like everything about you...It's just...my life is taking a turn, going in a new direction now..."

"But I do, Arionne. I do want to see other people. I do want to date other women."

"I can't do this anymore."

"This is really hard to say, but I have no more romantic feelings for you."

These aren't lines in a script from a play about breakups. I didn't find these statements in a google search. They aren't even from bad 1980s movies. I didn't hear them in a song or read them in a book. I didn't copy them from the PowerPoint presentation shared at some women's empowerment conference.

These are *real* words spoken directly to me from different men I've dated, wanted, and loved. Men I thought wanted me just as much as I did them, or at least I'd hoped they would. And maybe they did, but it didn't last. And when the curtain came crashing down to the stage signaling the end of our real-life love drama, it hurt. Really hurt. Really bad. These words were painful game-changers, watershed moments from which some of those relationships would never recover. In each case there was a wave of hurt that followed their, "I don't want to be with you" declarations. The loss was real. The shock was staggering. The pain, heart-wrenching. And the disappointment weighed heavily like a ton of bricks.

All of these wonderful men had found different ways of saying "Arionne, I really think you're a great girl, but I just can't be with you." Some added this consolation, "Well, at least not now." This was the common ending of all of my attempts at relationships. It happened so often that I began to talk to close friends about how I was quickly becoming the poster child for "Love Unrequited." "I love you, Arionne, but..." was all I ever seemed to hear.

At the end of the day, I just want to be loved. We all do. I'm convinced that's one of our deepest longings. We spend our lifetimes looking, waiting, hoping for that amazing, crazy, passionate, genuine love. (And some unsuccessfully pretend we don't want it). But, we sing about it. We make movies about it. We stay up late chatting with our friends about it. We take risks for it. We make sacrifices to keep it. We cry over it. We even write books about it. So when the person we dream about, crush on, go crazy over, that one who makes us blush, that one we desire more than anything or anyone else in the world, when that one *decides* not to love us back, it hurts like hell. Like. Hell.

The story I share with you here will focus on the latter part of my twenties, recounting my biggest "hurt like hell" moment. I can't tell you all the love stories of my twenties. Not enough time. Not enough space. Instead we'll focus on the most intense of my hurt, working our way through my healing process, not that your process will be exactly like mine. I just want to let you peek in and see that healing is possible; I know because I've lived it.

All I ask is that you let me be myself as I spill all my juicy details on these pages. Let me be the perfectly imperfect and fully flawed person that I am and receive me without judgment. This will keep me honest and our conversation rich. I wear many hats: daughter, friend, granddaughter, big cousin, minister, soror, preacher, coworker, and church leader, but here I'm putting all that aside and I just want to be the girl waiting and hoping for love, and your close companion as we explore together the ways of healing our broken hearts.

Now back to these fabulous men I've liked, wanted, and loved... Let me tell you that my experiences with them have been sometimes short-lived, often unfulfilling, and always full of let downs and disappointments. I wish that I could say this more positively, but I have to be honest. Even the Bible says that mortals who are born of a woman have but a few days and they are full of trouble (Job 14:1). And this has been the story of my love life. I have spent time with and dated some of the smartest, sexiest, most loving, hard-working, and caring men ever! (Yes, yes I have good taste!) However, for numerous reasons these relationships didn't work out. And for me, most of the break-ups were devastating.

A few years ago, I read this on my cousin's Facebook page: "There can be no great disappointment where there is no great love." She was quoting Dr. Martin Luther King. When I read it, I wanted to jump up and shout, "AMEN!!!" At the time I was right in the thick of a very tiresome and painful on-and-off again relationship that was fatiguing my heart like nothing else ever had. But instead of screaming like a maniac in my work cubicle, I simply clicked the like button, placed that insight in my pocket, and kept it moving. Those words of Dr. King were powerfully redemptive for me. I resolved that it was okay to have been disappointed because it meant that I had really loved.

Have I been perfect in loving? No. But I am still happy that I have. My pastor told me once, "Arionne, when you love, you love deeply." And he was so right in his observation of me. In fact, every man I have ever loved, I still love. Even after and in the midst of all the pain, let downs, and disappointments, I still love. The scripture really is true, "Love never ends." (1 Corinthians 13:8) It really keeps going, even if the relationship does not. Love keeps going. And I don't regret having loved any of the men I have loved, though it has certainly afforded me pain. There is no shame in loving someone. And we are never wrong when we *choose* to love.

Deeper reflection on this topic forces me to ask

questions about how my experiences with love, relationships, and hurt have affected me. Is there some measure of grace available to me after all I have been through in this area of my life? Is there some glimmer of hope? Even after enduring the disappointments over and over again, even after feeling low from striking out each time I get up to bat, is there any silver lining? Why, yes.

It may sound sort of cliché', but it really is true: Each hurtful experience, each journey through the healing process has and is helping to make me a better me. If nothing else, I have become immensely stronger each time. I'm tougher now; I can take more. I still need and rely on God, but I am stronger now than I've ever been. And each time I come to the table with more experience. I know what to expect. I've learned the stages of the healing process. I know how to get through the pain, how to overcome. Most importantly, I know how to care for myself during the process.

And that's what we'll spend time exploring here. How did I work through my own pain? How did I make room for healing in my life? How did I let God in *to do* the healing? And how *can you* do the same?

My "I love you Arionne, but..." stories happened all too often for my comfort. One after the other after the other. All along, I was thinking, "My God is anything ever going to work out for me?" Even after turning thirty, I'm still somewhere behind that ellipses... waiting to experience the real lasting love that I want. But somehow, I'm not bitter and am still completely hopeful about the love that is to come. The heartbreak did not win over me, I prevailed over it. And so can you... So let's get into this first, "*I love you Arionne, but...*" story.

CHAPTER TWO ME AND MIKE

"Who wants that perfect love story, anyway?...Who wants that hero love that saves the day, anyway? Cliché', cliché', cliché', cliché'..."

– Beyonce on "Part II" from Jay-Z's Magna Carta Holy Grail

It was a Saturday evening and I was super excited to be spending time with Mike again. He was beyond sexy! Even better: he was ambitious, hardworking, and had much swag. I don't ever remember being more attracted to a man. He had smooth chocolate skin, a very manly mustache, big beautiful brown eyes, and a stocky build. He used to make jokes about his stomach being kind of pudgy, but, honestly, it didn't bother me. I liked it. And I liked him—just the way he was.

We had known each other for a long time. We grew up in the same area, but we didn't have much contact back then. When I finished graduate school and moved back to Kansas City, we caught up with each other and reconnected. When spring returned, I was ending a very tiring, off-and-on, tumultuous relationship; truly, my heart just needed a rest. I was ready to be happy and free again, and the warmth of May had me feeling optimistic about life. Cindy Lauper was right: sometimes a girl just wants to have fun! And it's funny how the universe seems to respond to what you want because before I knew it, there was Mike.

He was a barber and entrepreneur, young, single, no kids—in other words, a complete anomaly. And did I mention fine?!?!?! I loved how he ran his business and how he was so committed to his goals. He was funny, a gentlemen, and active in the community. And again, sexy. So that twenty-five minutes or so I spent with him every two weeks while he cleaned up my eyebrows was pure heaven. I would sit in his chair, lean back and smile on the inside simply because I was near him. As he worked on my brows, we would talk about life, family, goals, and share stories about the past few weeks. This was the highlight of my day because I was seriously Little Kim crushing on him. Truthfully, I had no real plans to do anything about it. I was resolved just to enjoy our few moments together. When he'd finished, I would pay, throw on my shades, and leave. Until next time..."Bye Mike!"

One day I was in the shop, lying back in his chair, looking up at him. As usual, I sneaked a peak at the muscles in his arm as he picked the scissors up. He leaned in towards me to work on my brows and–in that semi-raspy cadence he talks with–said, "So Arionne, Ahemm" he cleared his throat, "I'm about to start taking two-stepping classes down at the Juke House on Mondays, and uuhhh I want to you to come with me. You know, be my dance partner?" Whhhhaaaaat? Was Mike asking me to a weekly date with him? Outside of the shop? If I'd known how to do the dance at the time, I would have totally jumped up and hit my dougie, well at least on the inside. Point is, I was excited. But rather than scare the man to death by shouting for complete joy, I simply smiled and said, "Sure, I'd love to. Sounds like fun."

That was on a Tuesday and time must have zipped by because the next thing I knew, it was 4:30 on Monday—time to leave work and head down to the Juke House to dance with Mike. He arrived twenty-five minutes late, but when he walked in and smiled, I forgave him. Our teacher was one of the most well-known two-steppers in Kansas City. Mike and I faced each other as we tried to pick up on the steps, laughing at each other's mistakes and enjoying the company.

After class we hung out at Juke for a while. It was a pretty nice club, known for their two-steppers, delicious Juke House wings, and good R&B music. I liked it because (back then, at least) it wasn't full of droppin'-it-like it's-hot 21 year-old kids hyped up on too much alcohol and booty music. Rather this crowd was more mature, they were Black folks of varying ages, who just loved good soul music and carrying on Kansas City's long-time tradition of two-stepping. That's my favorite kind of dancing in the world. It's not Chicago stepping; it's Kansas City's own invention, our slow dance, our groove. Our parents and grandparents had grown up two-stepping at house parties, school dances, and clubs, but the tradition was sort of lost on younger generations. However, it was coming back, experiencing a renaissance of sorts. And thanks to Mike, I learned how to do it. And whenever we did it, I enjoyed myself immensely.

Once we were at a party he threw, celebrating some of his professional successes. I was fly that night. Cute black dress, hair down and flowing, leopard pumps, red lips. Yes! I WERKED!!! (Even if I have to say so myself.) Mike looked good, too, like he always did. Black suit, black shirt, crisp tie, dreads back, yes. It was all beautiful. After he said his hellos to people, he came and got me so that we could dance—and dance we did.

Right, left, rock, rock, rock. Right, left, rock, rock, rock. His hand on my waist, he turned me, full turn, half turn. We got close, pulled back. We clasped our hands as our bodies moved together in perfect harmony. Slow jams blazing in the air, the DJ was killing it! You see, two-stepping is all about the groove. It's about how you feel—your confidence, your sexiness, your heart shows up in your movement. If you let it, the music will guide you into a place of total ecstasy as you dance. Ahhh... Nothing like it. It's pure unadulterated fun. We kept going, enjoying the music and each other. We were partners! And as it got good to us, we got closer, intertwining our fingers, a sign of being totally in sync. Our dance was always so relaxed, and still intimate. It was our thing—what we shared together.

But that first night of class, I had no idea what was to come over the next several months; I just showed up for a good time with Mike. Thirsty, I ordered a Coke at the bar and sat down to relax after class while Mike went to chat with an old friend. A few minutes later, he came and got me and I joined them on the patio outside. It was a beautiful and warm May afternoon, 78 degrees and sunny. The warm breeze blew across my arms, exposed by my sleeveless blouse. We sat there looking at cars and people pass on Vine Street, the historic Gem Theatre in our view. I remember we talked about movies (laughing about why in the world Tyler Perry would want to dress like a woman), mutual friends we knew, and even serious subjects like single fathers and the child support system. It was a lovely conversation on a casual Monday afternoon that carried on for an hour or so—a wonderful way to unwind after the work day. While deep in discussion, someone opened the patio door from inside the Juke, and I was interrupted mid-sentence by the most delicious soul food aroma that I had smelled in a long time. Embarrassingly, I blurted out these words before thinking, "I smell chicken!" My words were loud and devoid of my usual tactfulness, but honest and very funny! I giggled at my momentary lack of refinement. Mike looked in my eyes, laughing at my candor. His chocolate skin glistening in the sun, he smiled and asked, "Would you like to get something to eat?" Grateful that he'd reserved his jokes to spare me any further humiliation, I smiled back and said, "Yes, thank you." He opened the door for me, and we went inside for a little dinner and refreshment.

Amazingly, three hours later, we were still there.

We'd had dinner—those delicious Juke House wings, fries, and a drink or two. We'd stayed around to enjoy Soul Sessions, Kansas City's weekly gathering for young, Black, fabulous poets. They shared their freshest, newest verses about love, pain, and social uplift. That night, we'd even heard a poet from St. Louis named Xhibit, whose work was simply wonderful. Xhibit talked about love and being in love with his girlfriend. He was great. After his set, Mike bought the poet's CDs and gave them to me. (Smiles) We even saw a guy propose to his girlfriend that evening, and as fate would have it, she said yes! It was just a fantastic night. Dancing, music, good food, poetry, proposals, and great company. Our first class—and date—was truly memorable.

What I enjoyed more than all of that, though, was the vibe between Mike and me. It was the most relaxed, cool, and enjoyable feeling ever—the kind that makes you smile for no reason. It's a wonderful combination of: "I'm happy you're here," "I think you're cool," and "I wish we could do this all the time," all wrapped up in an "I kind of like you" warmth. It's fun, pure, and requires no words. We didn't have to talk, we could just be. No pretense. No agendas. Just be. It's something quite spectacular and rare—almost indescribable, but this is my best effort. It got so good to us that we indulged for some five hours that evening. So satisfying and unsatisfying at the same time, I wanted the evening to go on forever.

Until...practicality kicked in, interrupting our reverie. At 10:30, we called it a night. Back to reality. Both of us were surprised at how long we'd stayed. Sitting close to me at the table, Mike turned to look at me and said, "Can you believe it's 10:30?" "I know!" I replied in disbelief. So we got up and headed outside. He walked me to my white 1991 Pontiac Grand Prix (yeah classy, I know) and opened my door. He gave me a hug and cracked some joke about how short I was. I popped right back with a dig at his own height challenges. "Touché. Touché." he laughed. We smiled and said goodnight. I drove home, floating on cloud nine, feeling like I'd just breathed the freshest air of my life.

"I see you cross the room talking to some men. I love your mannerisms babe, the way you handle them."
—Jill Scott in "So In Love" with Anthony Hamilton

Sang, Jill. That's pretty much how I felt about Mike. I loved the way he talked, carried himself, and conducted business. He was direct, smooth, wise, and always a gentleman. I got to know more and more that summer as we continued to dance, laugh, and share every week. As the heat of Kansas City blazed on, there were movies, concerts, late night snacks, and a few parties we'd enjoy. It was fun hanging out over those few months, but after awhile, I was beginning to wonder where things were really going. So after we spent the night dancing at one of his parties, I'd decided I was ready to know. Summer was drawing to a close, but I'd hoped we weren't.

We sat down one night to enjoy yummy tacos at a

lively bar in the entertainment district called Westport to talk about it. It was Taco Tuesday and you could get three tacos for $2, or something crazy like that. We ate. We laughed. And after some small talk, I put on my big girl panties and asked what I wanted to know. "Mike, how do you feel about me?" In retrospect, it's funny that I asked that way. I knew he liked me, but he wasn't really a big talker so he'd never actually said it. He smiled, laughed nervously, looked around, and took a few deep breaths. His hesitation to respond made me nervous and I had the feeling he might not exactly say what I wanted to hear. The vibe felt kind of weird and his energy felt awkward and heavy, like he was about to say something he'd rather not say. He laughed even more nervously, and I wasn't feeling the way I hoped I'd be feeling in the moment after asking that question.

"Ahem," He cleared his throat and looked around some more, as if searching for the right words or perhaps a way to escape the moment. "How do I feel about you?" I could almost hear his heart beating. More nervous laughter. He paused, took another breath, looked in my eyes, and seemed to finally calm down. Resigned to proceed with the truth, he said, "I *dig* you. I think you're pretty. I think you're smart. I like your spirit, your attitude. I like the way you carry yourself. I damn near like everything about you..." His tone was warm and honest and his words, reassuring. "Okay," I'm thinking, "So far, so good. He likes me, nearly everything about me. I can live with that." Honestly, it felt great to finally hear those words from Mike, but inside I felt worried and nervous because I knew there was something else coming that probably wasn't so good. The moment was thick with tension. He continued, "It's just... My life is taking a turn, going in a new direction now..." He took a deep breath and finally let it all loose and said, "I have a baby on the way." WHAAAATTT??? LUMP. My heart sank, hitting the bottom of my chest cavity with a thud so loud that I was sure Mike heard it. My eyes got big. I took the deepest breath ever, feeling the pain struggle to make its way down my body riding the wave of my exhale. I was thinking, "Are you *kidding* me? He can't be serious. This cannot be real." Sighs and more deep sighs. I couldn't talk. There were no words. Suddenly it felt dark and even chilly. The sun I was used to standing in with Mike? Gone. The warm May breeze? Gone. All I could feel was pain. Another disappointment. I couldn't believe it was happening again.

There it was, "*I love you Arionne, but...*"

I listened to him talk, trying to keep my poker face in tack. I was stunned, angry, and deflated all at once. He'd said that he'd known for several weeks now, but was trying to figure out a way to tell me, afraid of how I would react. "I just didn't want you to be hurt." he said. He explained how he and the child's mother had "no drama." I interrupted, "Yeah, that's until she finds out there's another woman in the picture." He assured me that they weren't together and had stopped seeing each other months ago. But still, a baby? This was big. Not the kind of thing you work through easily. "Huuuuuuhhhhh!!!"

Later that night, I walked in my grandmother and mom's house completely irritated with Mike and the whole situation. Since it was so late, I stayed at her place because it was much closer to my job than my house, and honestly, I needed a little time with my mom while trying to recover from the bomb that Mike had just dropped. I couldn't believe this.

Here was something I found to be wonderful developing between the two of us. Finally, I was getting closer to having the kind of love I wanted. The best part was that it all happened so naturally! There was nothing forced or contrived. Our entire experience was completely organic. The funny part was that back in the day as kids, Mike and I ran in totally different circles; we were so different. We once talked about how neither of us would've ever thought we'd start liking each other. In fact, Mike told me that he felt like somebody had sprinkled some kind of magical dust over us that first night we hung out. He said he hadn't expected to catch any feelings, but he had. And so had I. Sure. I'd had a little crush on him before, but it was just that: a crush. I had no intentions on following through on that, but then we started going to class and BOOM! Out of nowhere, we started smiling and looking at each other differently, and before we knew it, we had this this thing going on. So I finally had someone to be excited about and so much to look forward to. Here I was ready to explore with Mike what adventures we could have together. And now there was a baby coming, one I was not carrying, putting the brakes on whatever plans I had brewing in my mind.

As I entered the living room, my mom looked up at me from the couch, donning her flower-patterned robe and colorful head scarf. She immediately sensed my sour disposition—as mother's tend to do. "What's the matter, baby?" I rolled my eyes and sighed loudly. "What happened?" she urged me to talk. I just shook my head and sighed some more. Still processing everything I'd heard Mike say, perhaps I wasn't ready to verbalize it myself. And I couldn't help but notice that lump was still sitting in the middle of my chest, heavy and refusing to budge. I sat down on the couch next to her, so annoyed I could barely move. Mom grabbed the remote and turned down the TV, bracing herself for what I was about to say. I saw a frown shoot crinkle lines across her forehead, her flawless brown skin shining in the white light cast from the light fixture on the ceiling. She listened. I breathed a few more slow breaths, and finally let the words roll off my tongue. "Mike has a baby on the way."

And there it was, as real as it had been at the restaurant. As real as the lump in my chest. I wanted to scream, but for what? It wouldn't change the circumstances or how I felt about them. All I could feel that day was anger and irritation because deep in the recesses of my mind, I knew that this would represent a major change in Mike's life. Consequently, the possibility that we could proceed on the path we were on was slim.

"Oh Miiiiiiike," my mother squealed with disappointment. "Huuuh," she sighed. She put her arm around my neck and said, "It's gonna be okay." I rolled my eyes as I thought about everything. After a few moments of silence and several heavy breaths, I blurted out, "This is stupid! Just stupid." I was highly annoyed that I was right back in that "I-love-you-Arionne-but" place. At the same time, as Mike's friend, I was trying to find some joy and happiness in this for him. I was hoping and praying he'd be ready for all the changes this blessing of a baby would bring, praying he'd be a great father. I was sure that he would be. He'd better be, because no matter what he felt or I felt, what he wanted or I wanted, this baby was coming. Nothing was changing that. I just had to figure out if there was still a place for me in all this. It surely did not seem like it.

Before our taco feast ended that night, Mike asked me to take some time and think carefully about what I wanted. "Take as long as you need. There's no rush. And when you've made your decision, then let me know. And we'll talk about it."

For the next two weeks, I carried that lump in the middle of my chest. I can't really explain why this thing was affecting me in such a physical way. It was strange. I'd never felt this and I'm not even sure I'm describing it adequately. All I know is that it felt like this huge stress center in my chest that absolutely was not moving. And I figured that it was going to be there at least until I made a decision.

Now you might be thinking, "Girl, what is there to even think about? He's having a baby with another woman. And you were *just dating*. Technically, he's not your man sooo... Why not get out of there while you're ahead?" And I hear you. That makes total sense, but the heart does not necessarily comply with the rules of logic. It does as it pleases. There is no switch to flip off and shut down your feelings, no magic potion to drink that will wash them away. And there is certainly no easy button to push here because there is nothing easy about the decision. When your heart cannot get what it wants, it can put on a strong protest. It does not give up easily— if ever at all. You just have to fight your way through the chaos as you weigh your options, praying and trying your best to make a good choice *for you*.

A few agonizing weeks later, I sat down with Mike to finally tell him what I wanted to do. I can't say I was completely sure it would work the way I wanted, but it was time to talk. I was ready to make my move, win, lose, or draw. So we met at Nara, a chic little sushi spot downtown that served the most delicious plum wine. It was just my luck that they were out that evening. It was probably a sign.

So we jumped right into the conversation. I told Mike that the news about his baby had really stunned me. I'd gathered from the timeline he'd presented that his child was conceived just shortly before he and I started hanging out. There was also the possibility that there was some overlap. Either way, it's crazy how none of these realities changed the way I felt. I still liked Mike, *really* liked him. That amazed me. The truth was there was a woman carrying *his* child, but my feelings were just as fresh and pure as they had always been. And for me, it wasn't about his success; I was attracted to the ambition and work ethic behind it. I was not impressed by his status or anything else he had. At the core, I *just liked him.* I loved how he was always such a gentleman. I always felt so comfortable and happy and cared for when I was with him. I could relax when we were together because I knew he had my back. It was just a beautiful and pleasant experience. That thing we shared was just so special and rare, and I wasn't ready to give that up.

So I told him just that. "This is kind of crazy, Mike.... because despite all of this, and everything you've told me, I still feel the same and I still want the same thing. I think we've got something special and I'd like to see where it could go. I realize this is not an ideal climate for starting a relationship, but I'd like to explore it if you would." That's the cliff-notes version of what I said. Much of that night is still a blur so I'm pulling out the highlights. I paused and sighed and waited for his response.

Mike started shaking his head no, and said, "I don't think we should do this. I've been through something similar before and I just think it's best we stay friends." And it was at that moment that I wanted to completely curse him out! I'm thinking "WTF??? If you didn't want to proceed with anything, why the hell did you ask me to take time to 'think about it???' " I was blown away. He went on to talk about how the timing was all wrong (which it was). He said he truly valued having me in his life and didn't want to mess that up. He was worried that if we moved forward with anything at this point, it would go totally sour. We would no longer be cool, and we'd both be left hurting. *Blah, blah, blah...* I thought. I reminded him that he'd already "hurt me" in a sense, but somehow my feelings weathered that storm. And despite all of that, I still wanted him. It was crazy! But even still, he was hesitating. He went on to say a lot of stuff that I could barely understand. All it amounted to was that he was not willing to move forward and that hurt *really badly*. It felt like someone had punched me in my chest. And *hard*. This was waaaaay worse than the baby news. It wasn't just, "I have a child on the way." Now it was, "I have a child on the way and I can't (I won't) be with you." A shot straight to my heart! I wanted to cry, but my poker face was on autopilot. So I just sat there and tried to listen as he talked, but I was mentally and emotionally checked out. Nothing hurts like the pain of rejection, and this was rejection in its purest form: I wanted to be with him, but he chose not to be with me. It hurt. And that hit I took in the middle of my chest eventually turned me completely numb that evening. I couldn't feel anything.

We stayed at Nara awhile after finishing our talk. It was done, but I wasn't quite ready to leave and perhaps neither was he. It was karoke night, so I signed us up.

"What the hell?" I thought. Still numb from the utter shock of the rejection, I sat quietly and enjoyed the entertainment. We laughed at all the people who could not sing and commented on a few other things. They called me up to sing and I gave my best rendition of Alicia Keys' "If I Aint Got You." How fitting because I sure didn't "have Mike" and wasn't about to have him apparently. I asked Mike NOT to record me with his phone while I sang, but he's hard-headed. I kept my eyes closed through most of the performance, and when I finally opened them during the bridge, there was Mike standing in my face and this super bright recording light from his phone shining in my eyes. He'd recorded me anyway. All I could do was burst into laughter and so did he. He made me sick! He could still make me laugh in the midst of all this!

"Mike?" The host called him to the microphone and he looked back at me and laughed. "You really signed me up for a solo?" "YEP!" I laughed harder. And when the music started playing, he laughed even more because he could not believe the song I picked for him–Marvin's Gaye's "Sexual Healing." It was hilarious! He sounded completely ridiculous because, let me be clear, Mike cannot sing. So to hear him squealing out those high tenor tones of Marvin's, "Baaaaaaaabeeee. I got sick this morn-ninnnn..." It was classic. He sounded a HOT MESS! And I laughed with every high note he hit! And so did he. We apparently needed that laugher to release some of the tension. This little exercise in karoke was the perfect distraction from the pain for me and served to fill in the awkward silences for both of us. There isn't much to talk about after the kind of conversation we'd just had. So the music again was our perfect escape, but we wouldn't dance to it that night. There was no shared energy to feel as when we two-stepped, no being perfectly in sync. We just sang and laughed our troubles away from the forefronts of our minds, at least for an hour or two.

When it was time to go, Mike walked me to my car. I stood outside the door for a minute in the crisp cold Kansas City fall air and turned to say goodbye. We hugged like we always did. It was an end of sorts. Sure I'd see Mike again, many times. So this wasn't a goodbye forever, but it was a goodbye to whatever I'd hope we could begin. As he put his arms around me, I could feel the numbness wearing off. And just before I turned to sit down in my car, Mike stopped and looked deep in my eyes. He'd never looked that closely before. It was like he wanted to see, to make sure I was okay. He wanted to see how bad this had hurt me. And I couldn't hide anymore. The pain started bubbling up in my chest and I felt the tears coming. I fought my hardest to push them back, but *they were coming.* And just before they came pouring out of my tear ducts, I believe that Mike *saw* my pain. He saw it all, everything I'd been trying to hide. I couldn't fool him. I was hurt and he knew it. Despite the laughing, my poker face, his awful singing, and everything I'd used to forget the pain that evening, he still saw it before even a single tear dropped down my face. And

I felt completely naked in front of him. He didn't say a word. And neither did I. But his big beautiful eyes said to me, "I see you. And damn...I'm so sorry." He looked right in and saw all of me—all the broken, hurting pieces, as I crumbled before him, struggling to hold it together.

And this was the only redeeming part of that evening: as I looked back at him, I saw that he really cared. He didn't try to say it, but he showed it—with just a look. In his face, I saw just how deeply he cared about me. I saw his concern. I saw his worry. I saw his regret. I *mattered* to him. He knew he had caused me some real hurt, and he wanted to know if I was okay. So he had courage enough to look at me in my face, and ask with his eyes, acknowledging my pain in the process. His eyes pierced me in the most loving of ways; and he saw it all–the devastation, the pain, the disappointment. There was no hiding. No man had ever looked at me that way before, nor has any since. So for just a few brief seconds, we both stood there before each other completely vulnerable. He saw my pain. I saw his love. It was incredible.

Unable to keep my composure a moment more, I looked away and sat down in my car and he closed the door. I tried to pull out of there as fast as I could. But as soon as my butt hit the seat, before I could even turn onto Grand Ave. and head to the highway, my face flooded with tears. I sobbed loudly all the way home.

. . . .

Mike and I would continue to see each other over the next several years. We celebrated a few very memorable birthdays together, danced at some more parties—sometimes so late that he'd stay over or I would. He was particularly helpful when I moved into my first place. He came over to assemble my TV stand for me, bought me some stools for my breakfast bar, picked up and delivered my dining room table. He looked out for me—a lot. And I appreciated him so much. We'd support some of each other's events. It was great. I was grateful for his friendship, but I always wanted more. I had to learn that just because you have feelings for someone doesn't mean you have to be with them. The timing was just wrong for us. It was all wrong. And even though I was angry and very hurt that Mike didn't want to pursue a relationship with me at the time, in retrospect, I know he made the right decision. It would have been a disaster.

My feelings for Mike never changed. They were always just as fresh and sincere as they were that first night we listened to poetry and danced at Juke. I'd always be hopeful that one day we'd get together and figure out how we could be together. "Maybe one day... he'll see." I'd say. "One day it'll happen." My heart never gave up. I'd always wonder if he would ever finally make a move. I'd move in and out of his space as I needed to in order to shield myself from anymore hurt. And I always got the feeling that Mike still liked me too, but our situation remained the same. A more serious relationship never blossomed. We stayed right there in the land of "I love you Arionne, but..." and sometimes that was a terribly disappointing place to be.

My experience with Mike has been one of my greatest lessons and questions in love: You don't always get what you want, so how do you live in the meantime? It won't always go your way, so how do you go on in light of that?

"Sometimes love comes around. And it knocks you down just get back up when it knocks you down."
– Keri Hilson, in "Knock You Down," featuring Kanye West and Ne-Yo from "A Perfect World"

CHAPTER THREE READY, SET, LOVE...

"I'm not ready." That's essentially what Mike had said. He just wasn't ready to move forward with me and pursue the kind of adventure in love that I'd wanted. You can wait and wait and wait. Hope and wait. Pray and wait. Hope some more. Wait some more, but you have no control over how love happens. There's no way to bend someone's will. And why would you even want to? If someone isn't willing to go where you want to go, it's best not to force it. It's better to just accept it. That can be a tough pill to swallow, especially when you really wanted it badly; but believe me, you're better for it in the long run. And somewhere in the aftermath of the let down that was Mike, I realized that I still wanted love. Real love. And if Mike didn't want to take that step with me, I was willing to take it with someone else who did. After some time passed, I moved back into my Cindi Lauper "Girls Just Wanna Have Fun" place. Though I was sad about the outcome with Mike, I kept living my life. There was much to be grateful for and much to look forward to. I was open for a new adventure with new possibilities. And it didn't take long for it to show up.

I remember the night I met him. It was a Saturday night in December, and my girlfriends and I were going to this event called "The Grape Gathering," a wine tasting hosted by a group by young black professionals in our hometown of Kansas City. It went from house to house twice a year and drew numerous other young, amazing people from around town. In Kansas City there really aren't many places for twenty- and thirty-something black professional folks to gather. There are clubs and some lounges, but after a few months, the crowd shifts and we find ourselves looking for a new place to be. So the Grape Gathering was usually an anticipated event that was well attended, as it filled a void in the social lives of us young and upwardly mobile black folk in the city.

I live a very busy life, working full-time, leading the youth ministry at church, and traveling for speaking engagements, so I had never had a chance to go to the Grape Gathering, but I had always wanted to. My friends always described it as a very classy and fun environment. There was no drunkenness. No fights. No drama. Just fabulous young black people being social, sampling wine, and sharing our brilliance with one another in great conversation. This particular night, I was determined to go and I was making all sorts of preparations to do so. I was trying to find the perfect nail polish because, according to my cousin Shelion, my nails looked a mess! So I was dropping in beauty supply stores to find the right shade of polish and the best tools to get my nails together, calling my bestie, Micki, on the phone to get her ideas. I kept harassing her, trying to sync our timing so that we'd arrive at the gathering at the same time. Normally, I struggle with punctuality and wait until the last minute to do everything, but that day I took time to get everything right: my hair, nails, outfit, make-up. For some reason, I was more excited than usual. As we were discussing nails on the phone, Micki said, "Girl, why are you so worked up about this?" And I said, "You never know, I might meet my husband tonight!" "Girl, BYE!" she said. We laughed out loud and hung up.

Despite my little joke, honestly, I was not looking to meet anyone that night. My schedule was already completely full of commitments. And I was in a really good and happy place, just living and enjoying my life. It had been a busy couple of weeks, and truthfully, that night I was after nothing but good old-fashioned-let-your-hair-down fun. I was excited to put on a cute outfit and head out to enjoy wine and laughs with my girlfriends.

And this little party was everything I had imagined and more. When I walked in, I was taken aback by the sheer number of young, professional black men that were there. When we go out, my girls and I never run into this many guys. It was like all the young single black professional men in the city were at this party. And they were clean cut, handsome, kind, and smart. Between sips of wine, we listened to music, discussed politics, and played a pretty cool remix of the charades game. It was fun. I noticed a guy sitting across from me during the game. He was cute and well-dressed, but my girls and I had only minimal interaction with him during the game.

As the night went on, some of us started dancing.

And I was a ring leader. Confession: I LOVE to dance. I always have and always will. In fact, I was up dancing without the help of my friends. We took it back, doing the bus stop, cha cha slide, and I might have hit my dougie—always a sign that I am in carefree-hair-let-down mode. I was really enjoying myself. I wasn't seeking anyone's attention, so I wasn't worried if I looked silly while dancing. It didn't matter what I had on or who was watching. I was just there to have a good time and that I did. My carefree feeling must've been apparent because my girl Sheriece looked at me, smiled and said, "You kicking it tonight, huh?" I smiled back and nodded yes. She seemed happy I was having so much fun. Now back to whipping my hair and hitting my dougie. It was a great feeling. I was confident, happy, and loving every minute of the experience.

The partying was getting so good that someone suggested we move to Firefly, a lounge in Westport, a major night-life district in Kansas City. Although I usually like Firefly, I wasn't really feeling the club scene, but I wasn't quite ready for my night to end either. Thankfully, I wasn't alone, and before I knew it Micki and I were headed to hang out with a couple of guys from the wine party at another spot, Harry's, which was a couple doors down from Firefly. I was the last person to find parking and naturally the last to make it inside to meet them. When I walked into Harry's, I saw my bestie chatting with Horace and his boy Phillip, who was visiting from New York. There was one seat left next to Micki, across from Jamaal. He was the cutie from the charades game, so I sat down in front of him, we started chatting and we immediately hit it off.

"Jamaal," he extended his hand. "Arionne," I responded, shaking his hand. He smiled and I smiled back. Caramel skin, muscular build, and a nice smile. His face had a boyish quality about it, but his voice was deep and sexy. I liked it. We small-talked for a few minutes about the party and all the fun we'd had. After a few minutes, he asked me that question I dread so much, "So what do you do?" I paused for a minute. I always get nervous at this point when meeting someone new. I've found that everybody ain't cool with dating or even hanging out with a minister. And to be honest, I don't always disclose that right away. I'm certainly not ashamed of who I am or what I do, but in certain social settings, it can make people uncomfortable. And I always want people to be themselves around me. For some reason, I decided not to hold back that night. So I swallowed my inhibitions and said, "I work for Social Security and I'm also the youth minister at my church." "Whew!" I thought, "That wasn't so bad." I waited for a few seconds to see how he would handle that. To my surprise, Jamaal responded, "Oh wow. That's cool. I'm actually on the youth ministry team at my church as well." Inside I was thinking, "Awesome!" This was a total win. So naturally, we kept going.

We learned that we had a lot in common. We both grew up in Kansas City and went to public schools. Our parents had divorced when we were just kids and both of our fathers were remarried. We both loved music and young people. We even both drove Honda Civics. It was funny. It had been a while since I'd met a guy with whom I shared this many interests, and the first time I was so open with someone so early about my calling and work in youth ministry. I was super thankful that my bestie, a very skillful conversationalist, kept the other two guys entertained with her brilliance and wit so that Jamaal and I had plenty of time to talk. (Shout out to Micki!!!) And talk we did. Our whole group chatted it up until 5am, ending the night with pancakes, coffee, and milk, having talked about everything under the sun. Jamaal and I decided to stay in touch so that we could get to know each other more.

I remember telling Micki that I was so glad to have met Jamaal. He was just really cool and great to talk to. I told her that I would be happy even if he just became a good friend. I was open to the possibility of dating, but I really didn't have an agenda. It was just really nice to meet someone like him and I was excited to see what would develop, but before I knew it, Jamaal and I were on date number two.

I remember bumping Common's "The Light" loud in my car as I rolled down 71 highway on my way to experience a bit more of this new adventure with Jamaal. Rapping along with Common and excited...

"I never knew a luh-luh-luh a love like this. Gotta be somethin' for me to write this. Queen, I ain't seen you in a minute. Wrote this letter and finally decided send it,

signed, sealed, delivered for us to grow together. Love has no limit let's spin it slow forever. I know your heart is weathered from what studs did to you. I ain't gon taunt him cuz I probably did it too."

Finally I arrived at Lucky Strike Bowling Alley in the popular Power and Light District downtown. I was super excited. The first date at Spin Pizza had been so nice, and like the night we met, we'd talked late into the early morning, sipping mochas at Starbucks. And the night of bowling would prove to be just as fun. My natural hair was blown straight, salon fresh, shiny and long, blowing freely in the crisp winter wind. I arrived a few minutes early, and sat down on one of the comfy couches in the lounge and waited for Jamaal. I played with my hair a bit and adjusted my clothing, touched up my lip gloss, ensuring I was looking my best. My look was casual: light makeup, cute sweater, skinny jeans, and brown knee boots—my heart pumping quickly, excited to be dating again. He walked in, tall, handsome, and clean cut. With a look of excitement on his face, he looked around for me, even though I was sitting right in front of him. When he finally looked down to see me, we both bursted out laughing. Grinning from ear to ear, we got closer and embraced. "Huuuhhh," I sighed on the inside. Those arms of his sure felt good. Probably a whole foot taller than me, he looked down at me and said, "You look great." "Thank you." I smiled back. We decided to grab some food at one of my favorite spots around the corner.

The evening was wonderful. I ate my favorite–boneless buffalo chicken wings with ranch sauce. We talked about our upcoming Christmas and travel plans, work, and church. Jamaal was really great company. We laughed at each other's jokes, shared smiles and stories about our childhoods. It was so exciting. The more I learned about him, the more I liked him, and the more I wanted to learn. He later totally dominated me in our bowling games but let me beat him one time. I don't have one athletic bone in my body. In fact when I bowl, I bend down like a 5 year-old and roll the ball between my legs, using both hands to push the ball down the lane. It's really pathetic, but he thought it was cute, laughing at my lack of skill. There was flirting, happiness, and pure fun. Before we left, he gave me an early Christmas present, a Starbucks giftcard! I thought, "Good job, Jamaal! Way to pay attention!" It's the little things that matter the most, after all. Definitely, the little things.

A few weeks later, it was Christmas Eve, and I was headed out to LA the next day. He would be out of town by the time I returned. So Jamaal called me to chat and touch base before our traveling went into motion. I smiled when I saw his name on my phone's screen. "Hey," he greeted me with that super sexy deep voice of his. "Hey! What's up?" my smile shining through my tone of voice. We talked about how busy our days had been: him shopping all day for last minute Christmas gifts, now staying up late to wrap them and my trying to pack so I could leave town.

A few minutes into the conversation, he asked "How should a man pursue you?" "Wow," I thought. I had never had a man be so direct with me before, but I liked it. I was almost startled by his question, so I paused for a moment to adjust before answering, thinking about what I really wanted. After a few seconds, I sighed and said, "I want to be courted. I want to go on dates, spend time together so we can really get to know each other. Make time for me. Show a real interest in getting to know me. I'll do the same. I think it's important to take the time and have good conversation. There should be no rush, just a commitment to make the time and see where it goes." He said, "Well, that's pretty reasonable. Sounds good." I sighed. That deep voice of his was a killer. I smiled on the inside and outside, happy and excited about the journey we were embarking upon. We talked for what seemed like hours about love, faith, relationships and the whole celibacy struggle. Surprised to learn celibacy was his goal, I was impressed. I thought, "Who the hell is this? And where has he been hiding?" Now granted, it could've just been game, but I can usually pick that out quickly. He was sincere. He was really trying to live out his faith the best way he knew how.

After we said goodnight, I drank egg nog and shuffled around my place for a few more hours, ironing and folding clothes for the trip. I listened to Ella Fitzgerald sing Christmas classics in the background, all the while feeling all warm and fuzzy from my chat with Jamaal. I was liking this new adventure with him, hopeful about what was to come. Good thoughts. Good feelings. It was all good. I was basking in this holiday-happy and the possibility of what I'd found as Ella sang on...

"Maybe it's much too early in the game. Ah but I thought I'd ask you just the same. What are you doing New Year's? New Year's Eve? Wonder whose arms will hold you good and tight. When it's exactly twelve o'clock that night. Welcoming in the New Year. New Year's Eve."
– From "What Are You Doing New Year's Eve" on "Ella Wishes You Swinging Christmas"

Well, Jamaal listened to my requests because by the time the new year rolled around, we were talking all the time and seeing each other two and three times a week like clockwork. We did every possible thing under the sun! We went to dinner, out to dance, browsed the aisles at Barnes and Noble, and we usually spent our Sunday evenings just hanging out at his house cooking, eating, laughing, and listening to good music. He had done exactly what I wanted. He *pursued* me. Finally! He made time for and courted me so we could get to know each other. And we were having a blast!

I remember one night we went to hear our city's new mayor speak at an annual Martin Luther King Celebration. We ran into the mother of one of my good friends and I introduced him to her. "Hi Mrs. J! How are you? Meet Jamaal. Jamaal, Mrs. J!" She smiled at him, extended her hand, looked back at me and said,

"Now, Arionne. Is this someone I should know?" As they shook hands, I smiled back at her, "Yes. yes, I think so." "Oh okay," she said in her signature high pitch vocal tone, looking with approval. We said our goodbyes and she disappeared into the crowd. Jamaal and I walked to the car, holding hands, and bundled up in the Kansas City cold. He looked at me and said "Wow. I'm someone she *should* know." "Yeah," I said confidently. He shook his head. "That's good to know. Very good to know." He smiled and opened the car door for me. I jumped in and we headed to dinner.

"Finally, it has happened to me right in front of my face and I just cannot hide it!"
—Ce Ce Peniston in "Finally" on "Finally"

"I'm pretty affectionate, Ari. Are you okay with that?" Jamaal had a tendency to catch me off guard with his very direct questions and the transparency with which he asked them. I sat on my bed that evening holding the phone trying to decide how I felt about affection. I had never really thought much about it. I knew that I wasn't really big on PDA (public display of affection), but I wasn't totally against it either. Either way though, I realized after a few moments of reflection, that I didn't really know how I felt about receiving a lot of affection from a man because I had never really had it before now. Whoa. What a sad realization: Twenty-eight years old and I'd never been with a man that was comfortable showing me regular affection. Most of the other men I'd dated were just too guarded, emotionally unavailable in their own way, or they just weren't the touchy-feely type. What kind of cold-hearted macho men had I been dating? But, if there was a reason to be sad, at the time I didn't feel it because Jamaal's energy and presence in my life prevented that. I was so happy he was there and wanting to be himself with me, displays of affection and all. I finally responded, "Well, honestly I've never had that before, so it's a new thing for me. But I don't have a problem with it. Just be yourself. That's what I want. Be yourself."

It's probably a good thing that he brought that up though, because the longer we were together the more affectionate he became. Seated closely together in one of those oversized chairs at Barnes and Noble one date night, his arm around me and my head resting on his chest, we took a love language quiz, digging through Gary Chapman's classic book. It was just a fun couple's activity that would help us understand one another's way of expressing love. Surprise, surprise, Jamaal's primary love language was physical touch and mine was words of affirmation. That quiz was so true to life. I wanted to constantly tell Jamaal how I felt. He wanted to show how he felt with touch. And for the most part this worked for us. We enjoyed that intimate moment as we talked through our quiz answers together. While eating up all the attention he was giving me, inside I felt such a comfort. It was a relaxed and resolved feeling, that finally it was real and working out for my good. We walked back to our cars that night hands clutched together, Kansas City's fierce cold cutting through my tights. Rocking my favorite wool houndstooth mini skirt, black booties, and my boo at my side, I felt beautiful, special, and happy.

Another night, Jamaal hugged me tightly as we stood in his living room. It was a Friday evening and we were having a movie night. He looked at me and said, "I'm so into you. You are really special to me." I felt a wave of excitement in my heart and all throughout my body. I smiled back at him, so grateful for the honesty of the moment. The cool part? This was just one of many moments like that. He never had a problem being affectionate, or telling me exactly how he felt. I had to admit; I felt the same way he did. It felt like I had never dated anyone where things we this well for this long. He said, "We really have to take care of this. It's so special and rare." I shook my head in agreement. "Yes, it is." He looked down at me, towering over me like he always did, with his right hand massaging the back of my head and scalp. "I think we should make this relationship more official. You know? Date exclusively." He looked into my eyes with such care. "What do you think? How would you feel about that?" And honestly, I knew this question would be coming up soon, but on the inside it felt a little fast to me. We had only been dating for a little over a month. And as wonderful as he was, it felt like we should take a bit more time and get to know each other even better. The fit was right. We got along great and we were having a blast, but no need to rush it, right? I looked back up at him and said, "I want to, but I think we should take some more time. This feels so right and so perfect, but it does feel a little soon to be in a relationship." He said okay and that he was happy to wait until I was ready. I was relieved that he understood, glad that my honesty was welcomed. He hugged me tightly again and said, "Let's watch the movie." We snuggled up on the couch for the next two hours while laughing at the foolery that is "The Hangover."

It was a few weeks later and my girls and I were out having dinner at a popular Mexican spot to say goodbye to our friend, Kris, who was moving out of town. There were at least ten of us there. We'd all been friends since high school. We'd shared years of memories together, school trips, dating disasters, college years, weddings, kids, you name it. So there we were deep in our laughter and usual antics, eating tacos and quesadillas, having a great time, when my girl Lexi looks at me and says, "Hey Ari. Where have you been lately? All boo-ed up and up under some new man?" Wow!!! My heart started racing. It's a good thing that I didn't have any of my beverage in my mouth because I would've surely spit it right out! I was caught completely off guard! I'm a pretty private person and I hadn't told any of the girls about Jamaal except Micki and Kris. Suddenly everyone was looking at me, waiting to hear the newest development in my love life. I was mortified. My face had to be displaying some weird mix between blushing, worry, and thinking. I'm no liar, so lying wasn't an option. It showed. There *was* a new guy and it showed all over my face. So I kept trying to evade the conversation, but Lexi would come right back to it... "So who is he?" I was smiling awkwardly, not knowing what to do. No answer. Some of the girls would start chatting about something else and then everyone would look right back at me. "Can we please talk about something else?" I begged. "No heffa! We want to know who he is!" I could've cried from sheer humiliation. My heart still pounding. This went on for ten minutes or so: Lexi pressing. Me evading. You may be wondering, "Arionne, what was the big damn deal?" Well, I really was not quite ready to answer questions about Jamaal, not to my friends. It was all so new and part of me didn't want to jinx it. I wanted Jamaal and me to be in a more secure place before I started sharing openly about us.

And there was another little reason. One night in a moment of pure transparency, Jamaal told me that he had taken one of my girlfriends, Kris, out on a date once, but nothing ever developed from it. He said he hadn't realized she and I were friends until after we started dating. In Kansas City, this kind of thing is bound to happen occasionally because the young, black, and fabulous social circle isn't but so big. Furthermore, she and I had talked about it and she had no problem with us dating. In fact, she said she thought we'd be great together. Her words had been very sincere, but she was the guest of honor that night. She was supposed to be the center of attention, not me. And honestly, I was worried what my friends would think—since she'd dated him first. The whole thing made me really uncomfortable.

In the end, none of that mattered because Lexi wouldn't give up. So I finally I relented. I spilled my beans. I took a deep breath, "His name is Jamaal." Pause. "He took Kris out one time, but she and I talked and she's cool with it." Much to my happiness, when they heard the news the girls were all terribly excited for me! Micki later told me, "Girl, you never talk about anybody you're dating to the whole group so this was major news!" I guess I hadn't considered that. They cheered me on and were all extremely happy that things were going so well for me. What a relief. No secrets. It was all out in the open and ultimately I was happy about that. All of them affirmed me in the most loving of ways; I needed that "you go girl!" celebration with my girls. It was so empowering.

In hindsight, I guess I really owed Lexi a thank you. She freed me from whatever worries and inhibitions I had created for myself. It's like it was becoming real. This thing was really happening in my life, the way I'd always wanted. And that's nothing to be ashamed of; it's something to cherish. When I left dinner that night, I knew I was going to say yes to Jamaal's prior question. I wanted to make things official too.

And in a few weeks, we did just that. Hanging at my house on a Sunday night, Jamaal asked me again. "Ari. Have you thought anymore about what I asked you? What do you feel about us being together? Being a couple?" Lounging on my couch, his arms around me, I looked at him and said, "Yes. Yes, I have. And, yes, I think we should be...official. Be a couple." "Really?" He responded as if he was surprised at my answer. And the tone of his voice was happy, innocent, and as honest as a child. I shook my head, blushing, "Yes. Really." He responded, "Wow. That's great!" and he looked deeply in my eyes. I gazed back. It was a precious moment, so much happiness and excitement between us and wrapped up in it. I just sat and basked in the joy of it all. It was finally real. What I'd been wanting for so long, I finally had it. And I was so grateful. Apparently, I had graduated from, "I love you Arionne, but..." to something much, much sweeter.

. . . .

I walked briskly through the mall, apparently on a mission to find something very specific, when my phone rang. "Hello," I answered. "Hey! What you doin' girl?" "Hey Daddy," I smiled, always happy to hear that guy's voice. "We're planning a really big Super Bowl party at the house on Sunday for the family. You gonna come over and watch the game with us?" "Aww, Dad. I'm sorry, but I already made plans to watch the game with Jamaal." "With who?" "Jamaal, the guy I told you about awhile back." "Awww." He paused. He wasn't used to my dating life conflicting with family events, mainly because it had been virtually non-existent—until now. "Aaaaight. Well, we'll get ya next time. Talk at ya later stink." "Love you!" "Love you too, baby." We hung up. He sounded a bit disappointed, and that kind of broke my heart, but I knew he understood. I had me a man now! Wooohooo! I'd waited for so long for this. And it was finally here.

Things were definitely shifting. On Super Bowl Sunday, Jamaal and I headed out to watch the game at this great sports bar with his childhood best friend and his girlfriend. It felt good for Jamaal to introduce me as his girlfriend. He placed his arm around me as we rooted for our teams. It was a great time. Before I knew it, Jamaal introduced me to all his friends. We all hung out once at Jamaal's place for a game night. I came over with my world famous nachos, helped him get all of his menu together, and prepared to host. It was nice to meet them all. We played charades, taboo, and some other board games I can barely remember. I was the girlfriend and it felt good. Finally.

It had been FOREVER and I mean FOREVER since I'd actually been dating someone around Valentine's Day. Literally, years. A few weeks prior to that annual love fest most guys hate, Jamaal and I had been at his house as usual on Sunday evening. He was doing a little work from home on his laptop and I was getting a few youth ministry tasks done. The place was quiet, with just the sound of our keyboard clicks and our breathing, but the room was full of warmth and happiness. After thirty-five minutes or so of working, Jamaal grabbed my hand and pulled me into his lap, "Let's take a break." "Okay," I said happily. We sat at his dining room table, his arms around me. He looked me in my face with those brown eyes and said, "This is really special. We have to protect it." "Awww." I smiled. "I agree with you. This is really special. And I'm having a great time. The best time I've ever had." He kissed me sweetly on the lips. We then went into this impromptu photo shoot, playing with the Photo Booth on my Mac. It was so much fun. We took over 50 pictures, making silly faces, serious faces, laughing at each other. It was great. Somewhere in between clicks, he looked at me and asked in the corniest voice he could find, "Will you be my Valentine?" then laughed at himself for how silly it sounded. I laughed too, and said, "Yes I will." We laughed even harder and finished up our shoot. And really it was the corniest thing ever, but a fun moment nonetheless.

Saturday night I heard knocking at my door and I got excited! We'd planned to celebrate the Saturday before, since Valentine's Day fell on a Tuesday. The time had finally come and I couldn't wait! I had spent the early part of the day at my mom's making Jamaal a sweet potato pie. He'd mentioned before how much he liked sweet potato pie so I wanted to surprise him and I couldn't wait for him to taste it. I wore a black dress that hit a few inches above the knee. It fit snuggly in the right places and had black sheer chiffon sleeves. Fabulous. Clicking along in my four inch heels, I went to open my door. There he was, handsome and smiling, standing there with my favorite flowers: TULIPS, a whole dozen of them! WIN! "Happy Valentine's Day." "Awww thank you!" he greeted me with a sweet peck on the lips.

"Happy Valentine's Day to you too!" I grabbed his hand and led him into my place, "Come on!" Super excited to give him his gift, I handed him the bag. He opened it. "Wow! How thoughtful of you, babe! Thank you." It was this really great cookbook he'd mentioned that he really wanted on one of our trips to Barnes and Noble. He loved to cook and I was so glad he liked it! Right before we left, he looked over on my stove and saw the pie, "What's that?" I smiled. "Oh that's for you. Homemade sweet potato pie." "Awww. Thank you so much! Wow." He kissed me on the cheek. We grabbed hands and headed out the door for dinner.

He was everything I had ever wanted in a man: smart, hardworking, handsome, kind, a gentleman, a Christian, and most importantly, interested in me. I just could not believe that I had met him. In fact, I wasn't looking for him when I did. It just happened. And I was truly grateful. It felt like everything I had been waiting for. I wasn't convinced yet that he was "the one," but I knew he was certainly a contender. Our time together was always so genuine, enjoyable, and fun. He courted me and pursued me, showing genuine interest. I couldn't have been happier.

While at work on Valentine's Day, I received a call from the mailroom, "Miss Williams, you have a package!" I was excited, practically skipping downstairs to see what it was, but I was pretty sure it was from Jamaal. It was a black and gold FTD box. When I got back to my desk, I quickly opened it up to find a beautiful arrangement of tulips of all colors: yellow, purple, red, pink. They were GORGEOUS! And I couldn't believe he bought me more tulips! So now I'd have some at home and some at work! It came with its own vase and a note that said,

To the most amazing woman I've ever met, Happy Valentine's Day! Love, Jamaal

My heart melted. Wow! Really? That's what he felt about me? I was overwhelmed with joy and blushing hard, while my co-workers smiled along with me. How lovely his words were! And the best part was that the feeling was mutual. He was simply wonderful. He was doing everything right. He was sincere, consistent, affectionate, and very grown man about all of it. I was such a happy girl!

Fast forward a few weeks later. My church was celebrating its Annual Youth Week. As youth minister, that week and the weeks leading up to it is always a marathon for me–lots of planning, long days, late nights, little sleep. Day after day there's all kinds of programs, kids everywhere, games, services, worship, more kids, money being spent, transporting kids around the city. It. Is. Nuts. But it's always a blast and it culminates in a youth-led worship service on Sunday morning. My dear sister Rev. Dominique (Dom) usually comes in to preach on Youth Sunday; my youth love her to death. Naturally, I invited Jamaal to come support me that Sunday and he did. He seemed to be looking forward to it. Dom and I exchanged looks when I spotted him walk in and find his seat in the back. He was handsome like always, confident, and low-key. She looked at him and smiled back at me with approval.

The service was fantastic. Dominique preached her heart out like always. My kids were blessed, the church was blessed. It was wonderful, and afterwards my church family headed to Kansas City's famous Gates BBQ restaurant to celebrate and dine together. It had become a Youth Sunday tradition, to end the week eating out together at a restaurant, usually Gates. Jamaal had agreed beforehand to join us for dinner. Of course, I failed to mention that nearly 30 plus people would be going with us, including my parents, my youth, pastor, and a host of relatives. And when Jamaal figured out that everybody and their mama was going to Gates, he was a no-show. Luckily, I hadn't mentioned to anyone that I would have my boyfriend with me. In fact, virtually no one knew that I even had a boyfriend at the time, just my closest friends and my mom. He hadn't even met my dad yet. That's a step I usually reserve for later, a few months into the relationship, after I'm sure we really have something worthwhile. In hindsight, I guess it would've been very awkward for Jamaal to meet my mom, my dad, my Pastor, my youth, and half my family and church family all at once—particularly since no one was expecting it. And that would've made it just as awkward for me. I'm such a private person and I'm not sure that I would've been ready for all the attention his presence surely would've gained us. And even though I understood all of this part of me still wanted him there, even if just a little.

He called me and said, "Hey. Are you in there?" "Hey babe, yeah I'm here. Where are you? Is something wrong?" He paused. Voice sounding less confident than usual, "I'm across the street. Yeah... I just didn't know that so many people were coming. I thought it would just be a couple of people, but don't worry about it." He took deep a breath. "I'll still come in." I could hear the nervousness in his voice. Not wanting to push him, and somewhat nervous myself, I said, "Well, would you rather not? I mean I will understand if you don't." "Okay, well yeah. I'll just go home," he said in relief. "Just come by when you're done with everything." "Okay." I hung up, feeling disappointed. I mean, as soon I'd given him an out, he took it. Apparently, he really *didn't* want to come. "What's wrong sis?" Dom read me perfectly well. "Jamaal's not coming." I answered sadly. "Why?" "Well I guess the idea of meeting and being around everyone was a bit overwhelming for him." "Well, I can understand that." she answered in a very reassuring tone. So, after a few minutes I shook it off, relaxed and enjoyed dinner with my loved ones. Jamaal later apologized, acknowledging that it was the first time he'd disappointed me, or as he put it: "really messed up." We talked through it and reached an understanding...I guess.

It was a Thursday night, and Jamaal came and picked me up at Shampoo By Salon Laron (my hair salon), as Jellae, my fantastic hair stylist, finished twisting up my hair. I saw that big (but very cute) apple-head of his pop inside the door. I was excited to see him. I gathered my things and we headed to grab dinner at Waldo Pizza around the corner. We laughed and enjoyed some of the best pizza I'd ever had. Afterwards, we sat and chatted for a bit. Jamaal initiated a conversation about how our relationship was going. We both said we were enjoying it and having a great time. I asked Jamaal what his expectations were for me. Somehow, we'd never really talked about our mutual expectations. He answered by saying that he wanted someone caring, reasonable, willing to be adventurous, all the things he said I already was. He shared that he didn't feel like he was really in love yet, but enjoying the experience nonetheless. This didn't really alarm me because I wasn't in love yet either. Honestly, I didn't have the expectation to be—not yet anyway. I shared that sentiment with him and we moved on with our night, laughing, flirting, and enjoying it completely. We went on to talk about taking a trip together to visit Washington, D.C. to see the cherry blossoms. He even invited me to go on a huge hiking-outdoorsy kind of trip with him and his friends. I was relieved that things were going well—that he was happy and so was I.

By the time March rolled around, Jamaal and I were in a groove. Our schedules allowed for us to hang out consistently on Wednesday and Thursday nights and on the weekends, and always on Sundays. It was so fun. We did all kinds of stuff. We were together a lot, sometimes spending the night when it got too late to drive. Over those few months, Jamaal had shown me the best time of my life! And I was truly grateful! So grateful, in fact, that I really wanted to show him just how much. I asked Jamaal to reserve a Saturday for me because I wanted to plan something special. The night before my bestie and my baby cousin were hanging out at my house. They helped me put together my casual, but very cute look. A peach and cream argyle sweater, jeans, and my Michael Kors cream-colored kicks.

That Saturday morning, I headed to his house to pick him up. I was excited and couldn't wait to treat him to a wonderful day. He was always taking me out, picking up all the tabs, but that day was all my treat. All day long! And I was thrilled. For me, this was a big deal. I don't always have a lot left over after I pay bills, so it was a sacrifice for me. But I didn't mind because I loved the way Jamaal made me feel and I was so appreciative for all he had given and for all he'd done over those three months. So I drove up to his place, and he came out looking as good as he wanted to look. Whew. For some reason he looked sexier to me than usual. The best part? He was going with me! LOL!

As we exited the highway, Jamaal was wearing me out trying to get me to tell him where we were going. He kept trying to guess, with no luck. As we got close to the Whole Foods store, he said, "It would be really awesome if we're going to a cooking class! Are we?" As we sat at the light, I turned to him, blushing super hard, "Yes, yes we are!" "That's awesome!" He got all excited. It's funny to think about it now because he was genuinely happy and it showed. Jamaal loved to cook. In fact, we'd spent countless Sunday evenings cooking in his kitchen. So I knew this would be the perfect date! And we had a great time in class, which was about all the cool things you can do with eggs: quiche, scramble, poach, boil, omelets; you name it, we learned it. He whispered in my ear during class, "Ari. Thank you so much for this." "I looked at him and said, "Aww, you're welcome." I felt my heart opening up more. I wasn't in love yet, but I realized in that moment that I was getting close. I was headed that way and I was okay with that.

The rest of the day we played around in the city, running in and out of stores. We ate frozen yogurt. We watched the Mizzou Tigers play and win the Big Twelve Conference title at a local bar while eating nachos and sharing spirits. It was his day, so we ate, hung out and went where he wanted to go, and we had a great time. It was all my treat and I was happy to share what I had. He had been so wonderful to me and this was my way of acknowledging that and saying thank you. And this was just the start. I had so much more that I wanted to say and share, so much more I was planning to give. At the end of the night, he kissed me and said thank you. I fell asleep at his house that night. Happy to be far, far beyond the land of "I Love You Arionne, But..." This place we were was cozy, comfortable, and everything I had been waiting for. And thank God because all the trauma of my past was finally behind. I was ready for love. And

I had it. Finally.

I woke up early the next morning and got ready to head home. I kissed him goodbye as I knew this would be the last time that I saw him for a few days. We normally saw each other three to four times a week, but our schedules would not allow it for that particular week. It would be a week before our next date, so I looked at him with a sad look on my face and the slightest sound of whining in my voice and said, "We aren't going to see each other all week." He looked back sort of surprised, as if he hadn't thought about it until I said it. We embraced and kissed like always. We smiled at each other. Then I jumped in my car and headed out to start the day.

Later that night, as I exited the highway by my apartment, I found myself thinking, "something isn't right." I did not like the way Jamaal had responded to us not seeing each other for a week, or better yet, didn't respond to me earlier. I began to wonder, "Is everything okay?" Deep inside, I felt that something was wrong, like he was bothered by something or felt somewhat disconnected from me. So I resolved that I would make sure that I brought it up to him soon.

It was Wednesday night and the week's activities went on as normal and we talked on the phone that night like always. Jamaal seemed normal. He talked to me about his day as usual, sharing his excitement about ministry at his church. I really had no concrete reason to think anything was wrong, but that nagging feeling inside kept telling me there was.

An hour or so passed and we kept talking. I turned off my bedroom light and laid in the bed as I listened to him. Then, in a moment of pure transparency, I said, "Jamaal, I kind of miss you." He paused for long moment, and said, "This is going to be hard, but I need to tell you something." With a voice full of anxiety, he slowly uttered these most awful words: "I have no more romantic feelings for you." My heart dropped. It was quiet. Very quiet. A long quiet. My mind went blank. I felt a sharp pain in my chest, and suddenly it was hard to breathe. I couldn't' believe what I was hearing. *What??? What the hell is he talking about*? I thought to myself. I was completely frozen, shocked beyond belief. Tears rolled down my face. I couldn't even talk.

Jamaal said, "Ari? Are you there?" More quiet. "I'm sorry," he mumbled. "Yes, I'm here," I said with my voice cracking and dripping with hurt. Pause. More silence. I swallowed deeply, "Are you saying you feel the same way about me as you do about your other female friends?" "Well, yes." Oh my GOD! The pain hit me like a dump truck. It was all too much. Where did this come from? How did he get here? How did I not see this coming? I was just about ready to fully let myself go and fall totally in love with him. Things were going so well with us. How did this happen? Why has this happened? I just can't believe it! It hurts like hell.

Then Jamaal asked, "I guess for you that means its over." I shot back a violent "YEAH!" Was he kidding me? There's a lot of things you can work on and improve in a relationship that's broken or struggling. Someone's basic desire for you is not one of them. In my mind, it was over. Period. The drastic change in his feelings assured me that there was no way we could move forward; he didn't really want me. He continued talking, telling me that he would like to still be friends. I listened to him in disbelief. After a few more minutes, I could not keep myself composed any longer. Crying and sobbing I said, " I can't talk anymore. I'm sorry, but I have to go." I hung up. And it all became totally real.

I laid in my bed and I screamed and sobbed at the top of my lungs. I yelled at God saying, "I didn't see this coming! Why is this happening?" I rolled around with my arms clinching my chest screaming louder than I ever had in my life. The pain was so heavy. Sobbing loudly, I rolled back and forth in the bed. I guess I was looking for some way to get rid of the pain. But there was no relief. Nothing felt comfortable. I was completely in shock. I'd known something was wrong, but I had no idea that it was this big. I thought maybe there was something we needed to talk about or work out, but I did not see a breakup coming.

Jamaal had been so perfect for me. He was everything I always wanted; if I had a picture in my mind of the perfect man, he was it. I could not believe that I'd finally met someone like him. We had everything in common. We laughed, shared interests, and had a great time together. We had been dating for a couple of months and it was time to finally settle into the relationship and enjoy it. When I'd taken him out and treated him to an all-day date the Saturday before, it signaled a turn for me. I was starting to really fall—in love, that is. And I wanted him to know how much I appreciated him. I wanted to show that I was so grateful for how good he had been to me. So for the first time, I planned everything and I picked up the tab. I was happy to do so and in my mind this was only the beginning of what I was ready to give. So this break-up caught me totally off guard.

What hurt more than anything was the fact that I thought I was finished with this kind of hurt. He and I talked early on about how great a fit we were together. He had told me "I'm so into you." And he talked about how we needed to be really careful to take care of this great relationship we'd been blessed with. I couldn't agree more. I was happy that FINALLY it was working out for me. So many times with other guys there were a million reasons why it did not work out. I was so used to hearing this, "I love you Arionne, but...I like everything about you Arionne, but...You are exactly what I'm looking for in a woman Arionne, but.." But! But! But! But!! BUT!!!!!! I mean I have been disappointed by men more times than I care to count. They had come up with every reason in the book as to why we shouldn't pursue a relationship: timing, too busy, focused on their career, baby on the way! Ugh!

But not this time. Jamaal had been totally different. After a month and a half of dating, he said he knew he wanted to be with me. So he asked. After a few weeks,

I finally said yes. So, I felt like I was finally winning in love! After all those let downs and disappointments, it was finally working. Jamaal made time for me and I for him. We were together a lot, had fun, and never really argued. He courted me the way I'd always dreamed. He was affectionate, respectful, and supportive. I loved every minute of it. I didn't know whether or not he was "the one," I just enjoyed him and the experience of being with him. Finally, I had the kind of man in my life I really wanted. So a break-up was the furthest thing from my mind.

Then Jamaal uttered the most painful words I've ever heard. Suddenly "break-up" was the reality of my life and heartache was all I could feel. I got up out of the bed and headed to the bathroom to try and wash tears from my face. While I stood in the mostly dark bathroom, I looked into the mirror and screamed some more. I just could not stop sobbing. Every time I thought I was done, more cries, more screams bubbled up from my heart and came wailing out of my mouth. I could hear my neighbors yelling through the wall, probably asking me to be quiet, but I just could not. All I could do was stand there and scream. It was awful. Just awful. I literally screamed all night.

Have you ever tried sleeping with a broken heart? It's no fun. I tossed and turned the entire night. I would fall asleep for fifteen or twenty minutes and then wake right back up and scream some more. There's something so intense about the ache in your heart that a restful night of sleep is just not possible. The sharp pain interrupts everything normal and your body just can't rest. So I went through this cycle all night: sob, then doze off (from pure exhaustion); wake up, sob, doze off; wake up, sob, doze off. I'm sure that I got a total of one and half hours of sleep in an eight-hour period. It was the worst night ever. I would not wish that experience on my worst enemy.

Completely blindsided by this, I was stunned, shocked, and appalled at how quickly it all happened. My fantasy completely unraveled in a matter of minutes. All it took was one phone call. One sentence and my dream transformed into a nightmare. I was hurt. Devastated. Angry. Restless. I had more questions than I could count. How had I missed this? Why didn't I see it coming? Why did God let me walk into this? I had no answers to any of those heart-wrenching questions, but there was something I did have. There was one little glimmer of hope. In the midst of all my pain, and all my questions, the one thing I did know was how to heal. The halls of heartbreak were not new for me. I had been here before, and I knew exactly how to maneuver my way through the corridors of my broken heart. Call it grace. I had no idea why any of this had happened, but I definitely knew how to get through it.

PART II SELF CARE IN THE AFTERMATH

CHAPTER FOUR PRACTICING ACCEPTANCE ACKNOWLEDGING WHAT HAPPENED

"You called yesterday
to basically say
that you cared for me but
that you're just not in love."
—Mariah Carey in "Breakdown" featuring Bone Thugs and Harmony on "Butterfly"

The road to healing from heartbreak starts with acceptance. Sigh...I know. Accepting the hurt sounds like a really ridiculous thing to do, but in this chapter we will see how acceptance is really the key that will unlock the door to healing. If you really want to move past the hurt of a broken relationship, you must start out by acknowledging what has happened. Let me elaborate.

The morning after the breakup with Jamal, I texted him as I pulled into my parking spot at work. I asked him to give me back whatever things I'd left at his house. I needed some closure and that phone call wasn't enough. I also sent a text to a few of my closest friends, my mom, and my mentor. It said,

Last night, Jamaal told me he had no romantic feelings for me. We broke up. I am devastated. I don't want to talk about it. Please just pray.

That text was a plea for support, and though it might seem like the natural thing for anyone to do after a break-up, it was far more than that. It was my first public acknowledgement of what had happened. I chose not to hide, but to be honest about what took place, and this is, again, the first important step towards healing: acceptance.

There is no way that you can heal from a broken heart if you do not first accept that somebody broke it. Acknowledging that it happened allows you to take the necessary steps towards healing. Think about your physical body. If you break your arm, the pain will lead you to seek medical attention. You'll see a doctor who will prescribe medication and tell you how to care for it. They will probably give you a sling or a cast and put you and your arm on the road to recovery. Weeks later after it is healed, you'll be glad you went to the doctor because now your arm is back to working order and you can go on with life as normal.

However, when it comes to matters of the heart, we sometimes have the hardest time simply acknowledging what happened. But don't you see that acknowledgement is the first step of the healing process? If you had refused to accept that you actually did break your arm, you would not have seen a doctor, taken medicine, or taken any of the necessary steps toward your healing. Eight weeks later you would still have a broken arm—and the pain it brought with it. This sounds ridiculous, right? Who would willfully walk around with a broken arm for eight weeks? I mean, it's so simple to go see a doctor and get it healed. But some of us walk around for months, years, (lifetimes!) with broken hearts that we have never sought to heal simply because we did not acknowledge that it happened.

As you read this book, if you really want to take action to heal the heartache inside, the first step must be for you to accept that it happened; someone did something that broke your heart. This applies whether you caused your own heartbreak or not. It does not matter if someone did you wrong, or if you did the wrong that caused the hurt. Acceptance places you in position to seek help and healing. No one can heal any hurt they will not admit is real. When I sent that text message to my loved ones, this was my way of accepting what had happened. I did not hide from the truth. It had happened. The man I believed had been sent to finally love me the way I always wanted, in fact, did not love me, did not want to love me, and was ready to leave me. It was real and it hurt terribly.

This is the hardest thing in the world to do because acceptance, by its very nature, will place you right in the center of your own pain. You will be forced to feel the hurt and live with the daily reality of what happened. There will be nowhere to run from the sorrow.

Acceptance forces you to face it.

I know. I know. This sounds horrible. Who wants to feel all that horrible stuff? It is so much easier to sweep things under the rug, shrug something off, or swallow it whole and keep it buried inside. People do this because they think these are alternative methods of healing or ways to just "get over it," but if you pretend it didn't happen, or if you try to force a different outcome so you don't have to accept it, you will slow down or prevent the healing process altogether.

I once heard Iyanla Vanzant say on Oprah's Lifeclass, "Whenever we fight against reality, we suffer." She is absolutely right on this. Here's the thing. When you suffer a heartbreak, the hurt you feel is real and it is present whether you choose to acknowledge it–or the event that caused it–or not. In the midst of the pain, you are faced with a choice. When you refuse to acknowledge what happened (break-up, infidelity, etc.) the hurt takes up permanent residence in your heart, becoming a part of you. You will carry it around with you everywhere and all the time. And there is no real relief from it, and no way to heal it because you won't acknowledge that it is there or how it got there.

Usually, heartbreak occurs because the outcome that you desired the most did not come to fruition. Dr. King said, "There can be no great disappointment where there is no great love." You loved. You believed. You were hopeful. You stuck it out. You were praying that it would work out the way you desired, but it just didn't.

Maybe it was a relationship, a dream, or a plan for your child's life. Whatever your aspiration, it went unfulfilled. The story did not end the way you planned. Somebody rewrote your happy ending without your permission. And the loss you suffered, the pain you felt was overwhelming and terribly heavy.

A contemporary example of one the tragedies that occurs when you do not accept a heartbreak is so-called "trapping." You know the story; it's a common narrative. A man and woman are facing tough times in their relationship and are headed towards a break-up. He knows it. She knows it. It's inevitable. And then somehow, the woman becomes pregnant. Now a precious a new life is growing in her womb, promising to inextricably link both the man and woman together for life. The woman is usually blamed for having gotten pregnant on purpose, although I've also heard of men intentionally causing pregnancies without the woman's knowledge. Of course any time a man and woman have sex they are agreeing to procreate; however, to alter contraceptive methods, and intentionally cause a pregnancy without your partner's knowledge is problematic, particularly for the sole purpose of trying to hold on to a relationship. Trapping.

This is a tragic mistake. Every time. It's tragic, especially for the person trying to hold on. I say that because it is an outright refusal to accept that the relationship is broken and, in some cases, over for good. If someone goes to the trouble of actually saying they don't want you, they probably mean it. I had no doubt in my mind that Jamaal was being completely sincere. As hard as it was to hear, and as hard as it might've been for him to say it, he told me the truth. And that hurt. It was a truth I did not want to hear, but it was real. Jamaal was no longer interested in being with me. That was the cold, hard, truth—and there was no changing that. The sooner I accepted that reality, the better off I was going to be.

STEP ONE OF ACCEPTANCE IS TO IDENTIFY WHAT EXACTLY HURT YOU.

What happened? Was it a change in feelings? Was it the break up? Was it is abuse? Was it infidelity? It might seem that this is obvious, but it could be deeper than you think. In my case, what really hurt wasn't merely the breakup itself. Jamaal didn't want me anymore. That meant he was choosing not to love me, so breaking up was what I decided to do. It was a natural and healthy response to the change in his feelings. But this also meant I had lost in love...again. So the "I love you Arionne, but..." saga, which I'd thought was over, was continuing. So for me the hurt was multi-layered: it was the change in his feelings, the breakup, the fact that this was another failed attempt at love and I still didn't have the thing I wanted most. And that was the deepest level of my pain, the reality that I still wouldn't experience the kind of loving relationship that I really wanted.

So as you think about your own pain, really take time to consider the many layers of it. If it was a breakup, ask yourself why the breakup hurt. It could be infidelity. Or it could be a shift in feelings. It could be some disappointing choice someone else made. It could be a combination of these or any other set of feelings and/or actions. Every situation is different and we're all affected differently by heartbreak, so there's no exact science here. Each of us enter relationships with different desires, interests, goals, and expectations, which affect how and why our hearts got broken. So you'll need to examine for yourself what exactly hurt you. This is powerful information that will help you begin moving towards your healing. When you know what hurt you, you can decide to accept it rather than fight against it. Since I was able to accept that Jamaal's feelings really had changed, I could decide to end the relationship, immediately.

I don't mean to suggest that heartbreak always has to lead to a breakup or end of a relationship. It does not. There are many people who decide to work through the hurt in their relationship and succeed in saving and restoring it. That is totally possible. However, in order to do that you have to recognize the root of your pain—what exactly caused your heartbreak. Once you have identified that and accepted it as real, now you are in a position to do something about it. You can begin making healthy choices for yourself that will restore your relationship. But if you won't face up to it, acknowledge it, there is no way you can address it. Acceptance opens the door to your healing process.

STEP TWO OF ACCEPTANCE IS ACKNOWLEDGING THE TRUTH OF A SITUATION AS FACTUAL AND IRREVERSIBLE.

This is key. Once you have identified what exactly hurt you, believe it. Don't try to rewrite the story. Don't try to change what happened. Don't ignore it either. It happened and it's real. Accept it. Anything else is denial. Acceptance has to do with acknowledging the other person's feeling, desire, or action that is usually in opposition to your own desires or feelings. It does not mean that you agree with the other person, what they did, how they feel, or what they want. It simply means that you acknowledge that they feel or desire something different than you do.

I wanted to be with Jamaal, but he did not want to be with me. And we all know that famous adage, "How can two can walk together unless they agree." So at the moment Jamaal told me, "I have no more romantic feelings for you," Jamaal was saying "Arionne, I'm feeling differently, so I choose not to walk this path with you anymore." This left me with a choice. I could accept this new development or not. To accept it meant to acknowledge that Jamaal's lack of desire for me was a real thing and then adjust my behavior accordingly and figure out how I would move forward. That's why I ended the relationship. Not accepting it would be to ignore or not take his words seriously or try to talk him out of his feelings. "Oh so what you really mean is...I don't think it's that you don't want me, it's really..." This is classic denial, which will keep you trapped in the hurt.

Notice however, that whether I choose to accept or deny what happened, it still happened. It was a reality. And no matter how much I wanted him to want me, I had no control over how he felt or what he wanted. There was nothing I could say or do to change his feeling. It was real. So it would not have been wise for me to fight this reality. That would be wasted energy and time, prolonging my pain. Bottom line? Jamaal didn't want me and I had no way of forcing him to.

You may ask, "but isn't it possible that things could turn around? Can't people change their minds? Can't these hurtful situations end in reconciliations, make-ups, etc?" To that I respond with an emphatic, "YES!" You're right. Jamaal could have called me weeks or even a year later and said, "Ari. I was wrong. I really do want to be with you. I was just upset about...I was scared..." We could have talked through all of it, fixed what was broken, reconciled, and rode off into the proverbial sunset. So can situations be reversed? Yes, but we have no control over that. Things could change, but we have no actual power to change them. That's why it's healthy to accept the truth as irreversible. When we refuse to accept what happened, it's because we think we can create a newer, happier ending for ourselves. Don't fall for this, convincing yourself that you can alter that hurtful event and force a different outcome. You cannot. This simply does not work.

Practicing acceptance requires us to relinquish our efforts to control the outcome.

LOSE CONTROL IT IS WHAT IT IS

A huge part about acceptance is distinguishing between what you have control over and what things you don't. You really can't do anything to force anyone to be with you, to feel a certain way, or to be anybody but who they are. When it comes to matters of the heart, life is completely volatile. You have no idea what is going on within the mind and heart of another person. And there really is no way to make them want anything. They have a will just like you do. They want what they want. And sometimes their wants change: what they desired previously, they no longer desire (i.e. Jamaal). And we have zero control over that. Of course there are those people who do manipulative things to get what they want or to achieve a desired end, even in relationships. But if it's forced, if it's manipulated, if it's anything but willful, organic, and natural, do you really want it? I mean, is that what you wanted in the first place? Probably not.

Consider the earlier "trapping" example. Deciding to have a child in order to save a relationship is really an attempt to control the other person, to stop them from leaving. The thinking is that "if I have his baby, he'll still be in my life." But he won't be in your life the way you want him to be. She might be your child's mother, but not necessarily your woman. What a false sense of control that is. The problem was not that you needed a baby, the problem was that your relationship was broken; it's what needed to be healed. And the truth is that if you had just accepted (identified and acknowledged) whatever heartbreak occurred in the context of the relationship, causing things to sour, you're in position to possibly heal the relationship. Instead, an attempt to control may have prevented that possibility of restoring the relationship permanently.

The only thing you have control over is your own behavior. You can't make anyone feel anything anymore than you can make yourself feel something. You don't even have control over how *you* feel, but you do have control over the choices you make. This is where the mind has to guide the heart. At the onset of a heartbreak, we always have a choice. I recommend we choose acceptance, which puts us on a path to healing.

THE DANGERS OF DENIAL

In this chapter I've mentioned denial several times because it's the polar opposite of acceptance. Either you accept the truth as it is or you're in denial. And sometimes, we float back and forth between the two. (That's totally normal by the way.) And if we're honest, we've all had our moments when we've poked our head inside denial's lush lounges of blissful ignorance and stepped in for a while to enjoy its comforts. There we can ignore the hurt, wish it away, and shield ourselves from the pain—or so we think. But we shouldn't take up residence there because it's just a fantasy. It's not real; there's no security or future in it. Meanwhile, below the surface of our facades and masquerades, our deepest pain resides. Those pains are harmful if ignored. Denial is a very dangerous place to be for a lot of reasons. I'll elaborate.

Denial is dangerous mainly because it grows from and cultivates deception. First of all, when you won't acknowledge that your heart was broken, you aren't being honest with yourself about your hurt or the circumstances that caused it. This forces you to create some alternative false storyline in your own mind about your situation. In other words, you actually start lying to yourself about how you feel, what the other person feels, what happened, etc—denial. Naturally, your actions follow suit, resulting in delusional and irrational behavior. You will start making decisions in accordance with the lies you've told yourself, completely oblivious to reality. Your ability to make healthy choices is totally handicapped by the illusions you've created. You throw all your energy into fighting for the outcome you want or pretending you already have it, but none of it is real and it never was.

Meanwhile your pain, which *is* real, is left totally unattended. For some, that heartache is above the surface on display for everyone around to see and it's a painful sight to witness. This is the person who causes scenes, acts out publicly, and will willingly make a fool of themselves (not in a good way). For others, the pain brews quietly below the surface like a volcano, with a propensity to erupt at any given time. Some people fluctuate between the two extremes. In both cases, by refusing to be honest with yourself, acknowledging your pain, you actually allow it to grow. It becomes a part of you, hardening your heart, producing unhealthy fruit in your life like bitterness, rage, and insecurity. Pain that is ignored can change who you are, and steal your joy and zest for life, robbing you of your future, your happiness, and your greatness.

Over time this raw, unhealed pain has the potential to take on a life of its own. In the worst cases, it rises up powerfully, pushing people to do harmful things to themselves and others. In this awful state, the pain is now actually controlling the person, rather than them managing and healing their pain. I am convinced that so many of our urban centers are plagued with violence because people are hurting with no way of coping and no hope for healing their own hurt. In this way, we see the incredible deceptive power of denial. Hurting people act out violently when they don't see a way out. Hurting people, hurt people, as the old adage goes. But there's always a potential for healing our hurt, we just first have to acknowledge it, so we can move past it.

Too often, though, we choose not to move past our hurt by staying stuck in denial. And that denial can play out in a number of ways. Sometimes we fight against the truth of our circumstances, desperately trying to rewrite the ending in our favor because we are convinced this will alleviate our pain. We reason that if we could just get the result we want, we'll feel better. We think *that* will heal us. Others of us simply ignore the hurt, and bury it deep inside, pretending it's not there. We reason, "if I just ignore this, it will go away. Time heals all wounds. It'll be fine." This is a complete lie; nothing could be further from the truth. If we believe these tactics will work, we deceive ourselves. Not being honest with yourself about your pain and your circumstances is always a losing strategy. It won't allow for healing because you can't deal with anything you won't face.

As a result our hurts continue to fester, growing along with us as we journey in life. Here we see how denial actually serves to prolong our pain. Since we refuse to acknowledge it, we hold on to it, and it can become a part of us. We take it with us into all of our relationships—romantic, platonic, familial, and professional. When we interact with friends, loved ones, and colleagues they encounter our pain along with all of our other qualities. Our unattended hurts can even manifest themselves in our physical bodies, literally making us sick. All the while, we think we're coping. We think we've gotten rid of the pain or at least we've hidden it from view; when in fact, it's still there on display for all to see. Do you see how powerfully deceptive denial is? Just because we won't acknowledge our heartbreak doesn't mean it's not real. We think by ignoring the truth we are escaping our pain, when in reality we are giving it life, and allowing it to stay around.

Ultimately, when we choose denial over acceptance, we are choosing not to heal. So much of what happens in the aftermath of a heartbreak is in our hands. No we may not have been able to prevent the heartbreak. And no we cannot go back and redo any of our prior actions. We cannot change the past, but we can decide how we will live in light of it. Denial is a deceptive downward spiral that does more damage to us than anyone else. It keeps us trapped squarely in the arms of our heartbreak, unable to free ourselves from its powerful grip, but acceptance is our route of escape. By acknowledging what happened and how we feel about it, we position ourselves to do something about it. When we're honest about what we went through, we can let all those hurts buried deep inside rise to the surface to get much needed air and light. There they can breathe and be seen. Now out in the open, we can deal with those hurts.

. . . .

At the end of the day, this is about choice. Will you accept what happened or will you live in denial as if it didn't? When you think about your past hurt, consider how you responded. Did you look your heartbreak squarely in the face? Did you acknowledge it? Did you identify exactly what hurt you? Did you accept, fight it, or ignore it? And how did that affect your behavior and decision-making? Your health? Your happiness? Perhaps it's still fresh for you and you're in the midst of heartbreak. Either way, you're in great position to choose acceptance over denial.

What choice will you make? Perhaps you decide to fight for your relationship. That's perfectly okay, but you shouldn't be doing so alone. Both people have to be willing to accept and examine the hurt and the events that caused it, working together towards your healing. It could be that you know you need to end a relationship, but won't because of your denial, because of your fear of a new life without the person. Perhaps you are suffering from the hurt of being abandoned by a parent and you have buried that hurt deep inside. Though it hurts, you can acknowledge even that and then begin to move forward. Take notice of what you have control over and what you don't. Acceptance is a life giving-choice you can make at any time. It's the beginning of your road to healing. I urge you to start making choices that are healthy for you. You are worthy of it. You don't have to stay broken and hurt. Choose life by looking your pain and the event that caused it in the face. This sets you up for the healing that you so desperately want and need. Be patient with yourself and start making choices that lead to healing.

When a heartbreak occurs there is always a struggle between the heart and the mind, especially early on. This is natural. The mind can more easily accept what happened as fact, but the heart puts on a strong protest. Consider the example of a breakup. You know in your mind that the breakup happened, but your heart on the other hand wanted this relationship. You were ready and committed yourself to being together. And since the heart gave it a go, your mind followed suit. However, when the break up happened, the mind may have understood, but the heart is much harder to convince. So when we talk about acceptance, we are really talking about resolving the tension within yourself between your heart and your mind. The process is very trial and error. It's tough. We will not always get it right. And we won't learn all the lessons acceptance has to teach us at once. Some of the lessons come over time. It's a journey.

Now I don't mean to present this as if it's easy to do. It's not. The truth is we all struggle through all of this. Acceptance is a daily choice. We may be able to accept the heartbreak just fine today, but not so much tomorrow. So some days will be better than others. And that is okay. Don't beat yourself up when you fall down. Facing up to the happenings of your life, good and bad, will be a difficult task. It may even require you to take responsibility for your part in what happened. Heartbreaks are complicated events. There's multiple layers of hurts and a plethora of cause and effects involved. And it's just not easy to work through. It is difficult work.

Because acceptance is difficult, you should always reach out to your resources for support; this work is too hard to do all alone. You probably have more resources than you know. Here are some examples. Nurture your prayer life. (We'll return to this topic later). Stay in touch with close friends and family. Counseling and therapy are also options you should strongly consider. In the midst of one of the most difficult times of my life, I went to therapy for the first time and I found it incredibly helpful. If nothing else, I had one person who would sit and listen to me once a week. At the time my mother had just had a stroke, and I was in the midst of fighting for the life of a very tumultuous relationship. My pain was real and I needed help processing all of it. So I went to therapy. It did wonders. I know there are stigmas around seeking support for mental health; it's often seen as an option for the weak and helpless. Some would even suggest that doing so shows a lack of faith in God. I contend that choosing your health and wellness over pain, to dare to make a change in your life by seeking some help, actually makes you strong. It's not a cowardly choice, it's a courageous, faith-filled one.

"So what do you do when somebody you're so devoted to suddenly just stops loving you?
Do you cling to your pride and sing "I Will Survive?"
Do you lash out and say, "How dare you leave this way?"
Do you hold on in vain til they just slip away?"
–Mariah Carey in "Breakdown" featuring Bone, Thugs, and Harmony from "Butterfly"

CHAPTER FIVE PRACTICING HONESTY BEING TRANSPARENT IN YOUR PAIN

"But Tamar put ashes on her head, and tore the long robe that she was wearing; she put her hand on her head, and went away crying aloud." ***2 Samuel 13:19***

This is the only redemptive verse I find in the story of Tamar, daughter of King David. 2 Samuel 13 describes the circumstances around the domestic and sexual violence Tamar experiences at the hand of her own family. It is a horrifying tale to read and imagine, but I'm certain far more terrifying for her to have lived. Hers is a story of lust, deception, betrayal, sibling rivalry, family and generational turmoil, vengeance, murder, and rape. And as difficult as her tale is to read, it is important for us to do so because Tamar stands out amongst other biblical characters. Despite being victimized by a close relative and doomed to a future of desolation, somehow Tamar's lasting impression is one of strength, courage, and honesty. In what were probably the darkest moments of her life, she teaches us the way of healing so that we may free ourselves from the pain that seeks to entrap and destroy us.

"Some time passed. David's son Absalom had a

beautiful sister whose name was Tamar; and David's son Amnon fell in love with her. Amnon was so tormented that he made himself ill because of his sister Tamar, for she was a virgin and it seemed impossible to Amnon to do anything to her. But Amnon had a friend whose name was Jonadab, the son of David's brother Shimeah; and Jonadab was a very crafty man. He said to him, "O son of the king, why are you so haggard morning after morning? Will you not tell me?" Amnon said to him, "I love Tamar, my brother Absalom's sister." Jonadab said to him, "Lie down on your bed, and pretend to be ill; and when your father comes to see you, say to him, "Let my sister Tamar come and give me something to eat, and prepare the food in my sight, so that I may see it and eat it from her hand.' " So Amnon lay down, and pretended to be ill; and when the king came to see him, Amnon said to the king, "Please let my sister Tamar come and make a couple of cakes in my sight, so that I may eat from her hand." Then David sent home to Tamar, saying, "Go to your brother Amnon's house, and prepare food for him." So Tamar went to her brother Amnon's house, where he was lying down. She took dough, kneaded it, made cakes in his sight, and baked the cakes. Then she took the pan and set them out before him, but he refused to eat. Amnon said, "Send out everyone from me." So everyone went out from him. Then Amnon said to Tamar, "Bring the food into the chamber, so that I may eat from your hand." So Tamar took the cakes she had made, and brought them into the chamber to Amnon her brother. But when she brought them near him to eat, he took hold of her, and said to her, "Come, lie with me, my sister." She answered him, "No, my brother, do not force me; for such a thing is not done in Israel; do not do anything so vile! As for me, where could I carry my shame? And as for you, you would be as one of the scoundrels in Israel. Now therefore, I beg you, speak to the king; for he will not withhold me from you." But he would not listen to her; and being stronger than she, he forced her and lay with her. Then Amnon was seized with a very great loathing for her; indeed, his loathing was even greater than the lust he had felt for her. Amnon said to her, "Get out!" But she said to him, "No, my brother; for this wrong in sending me away is greater than the other that you did to me." But he would not listen to her. He called the young man who served him and said, "Put this woman out of my presence, and bolt the door after her." (Now she was wearing a long robe with sleeves; for this is how the virgin daughters of the king were clothed in earlier times.) So his servant put her out, and bolted the door after her. But Tamar put ashes on her head, and tore the long robe that she was wearing; she put her hand on her head, and went away, crying aloud as she went. Her brother Absalom said to her, "Has Amnon your brother been with you? Be quiet for now, my sister; he is your brother; do not take this to heart." So Tamar remained, a desolate woman, in her brother Absalom's house.[1]

Can you imagine the pain of this woman? First of

1 2 Samuel 13: 1-20, New Revised Standard Version.

all she was a woman in ancient patriarchal Israel, which meant she had very little power. Much of her life and all of her activities would have been controlled by the men around her, her father and brothers. And so she would have spent much of her young life with other maidens (young, unmarried virgins) until it was time for her to marry. Tamar wasn't just any maiden though, she was a princess so she was especially prized.[2] She even wore a white garment that signified her virginity.[3] Her destiny was sure to lead to a very carefully arranged marriage, most likely to a wealthy, respected suitor, perhaps a royal himself.[4] Her only duty was to remain a virgin until that time came. This would ensure her value when it was time to marry and maintain great honor for her family, particularly her father. The marriage would more than likely be some smart political move for her family. Before any of that vision could come to pass, though, tragedy rose up in her family, rewriting the ending of her story.

Unbeknownst to Tamar, her half-brother Amnon, had fallen in lust with her. This lust burned in him so deeply that it made him sick, and his crafty friend, Jonadab, noticed that something was wrong. When he inquired, Amnon admitted that he wanted his sister

---

2 Frymer-Kensky, Tikva. *Reading The Women In The Bible.* New York: Schocken, 2002,158, Kindle.

3 Birch, Bruce C. New Interpreter's Bible Complete Twelve Volume Commentary: 2 Samuel. DVD-ROM. Nashville: Abingdon Press, 2002.

4 Frymer-Kensky, Ibid, 158.

Tamar but saw no way that he could be with her. Crafty man that he was, Jonadab plotted a way for Amnon to have sex with Tamar. It involved faking an illness, tricking King David, and requesting Tamar to come and care for him. Amnon asked the King to send Tamar to care for him, the King sent her, and she went. [5]

Tamar had no idea that when she arrived, her brother had planned to rape her. She prepared the food as he requested and he sent all the servants out of the room. Once they were alone, he grabbed a hold of her and commanded, "come lie with me my sister." At the moment, realizing what he really desired, Tamar protested strongly and pleaded with him not to "force her." She even suggests that the King would let them marry if he would just ask. Though incest was not commonly practiced in Israel, she reasoned that if anyone had the power to permit it, the King could.[6] In her mind, this alternative would be better than rape! Anything would be better than this! Her words do not stop him though; he refuses to listen and overpowers her and rapes her.

Then this disgusting tale takes quite an unexpected turn. Afterwards, the text says that Amnon's love for Tamar transformed into utter hatred. Unable to face what he has done,[7] Amnon tells her to "Get out!" What

5 Trible, Phyllis. Texts of Terror: Literary Feminist Readings of Biblical Narratives. Philadelphia: Fortress Press, 1984, Kindle, location 574.

6 Frymer-Kensky, Reading The Women In The Bible, 162.

7 Birch, Bruce C. Ibid, 2 Samuel 13:1 Commentary, 13:15-19.

in the world? Somehow Tamar finds strength to raise her voice in protest again. "No, my brother; for this wrong in sending me away is greater than the other that you did to me." Apparently, she thought there was some way to still fix this. Again he doesn't listen. She is thrown out and he instructs his servant to bolt the door behind hers.

It is almost surreal. Tamar's life has been totally transformed in a matter of minutes. I cannot imagine the overwhelming pain and grief Tamar experienced here. First of all, she was raped. This meant that her status as a young virgin princess ended violently and suddenly. Whatever hopes she or her family had for her to marry and bear children were shot to death. No one would want to marry her now. In taking her virginity, Amnon also snatched away whatever little value, honor, and prestige the patriarchal culture afforded the virgin princess. It was already a very limited, very controlled path she was to live, and now even that was taken away. Amnon not only stole her youthful innocence, but he also stole her joy and the future as she knew it.

What's worse? It was her own brother who robbed her of these things. The very brother who had a duty to protect her honor and keep her safe from violence actually enacted violence upon her. She was not out in the fields or in the city, she was at her brother's house where she should have been completely safe. Moreover, when her father learned the news, we are told he was angry, but he took no action against Amnon.

Finally, perhaps the most painful of all that has

happened, is that after Amnon, her brother, has violated her and taken her future away from her, he throws her out her like the trash. "Get up and go!" he yells. Most contemporary translations use, "Get that woman out of here," but the Hebrew does not make reference to her as a woman. It literally says, "Send, please, *that* away from me."[8] She's no longer a person, perhaps never was a person in Amnon's eyes. She was only an object to be manipulated and controlled for his pleasure and then dismissed immediately afterwards. How hurtful. Her own brother doesn't value her life, nor see her personhood and certainly not her pain. He shows no regard for how his violent act has destroyed her and indeed broken her heart. In fact, the narrator said he "hated her," as if she is to blame for what he did. It is truly unbelievable and had to be utterly devastating to every part of her heart, mind, body, and soul.

In the next scene, Tamar emerges from her brother's house and takes swift, bold, and powerful action that makes her quite the inspiring character. Overcome with grief, Tamar rips her gown, places ashes on her head, puts her hands on top of her head and walks down the street crying loudly. In so doing, Tamar is performing an act of lament. This kind of action was customary for those mourning the death or seeing the ruin of their city or nation. I love the fact that Tamar re-appropriated this practice and grieved the loss of her own honor and future. Let's look closer at her actions to find incredible

8 Frymer-Kensky, *Ibid*, 164.

meaning and power.

First she, rips her gown—the one that signifies her virginity. This makes the statement, "I am no longer who I once was." She is boldly and publicly testifying to the fact that her days as a virginal maiden are over, along with whatever future she had wrapped up in them. Here, we find in Tamar's action a true example of acceptance. She is not condoning the violence she suffered at her brother's hand, but rather she is acknowledging what happened to herself, and to her community. Next she places ashes on her head, a sign of death and mourning. She'd lost so much so certainly mourning was a natural response for her. Her life as she knew it was completely over.

Then she places her hands on her head. Why would she do that? There was a law in neighboring Assyria where a woman unknowingly tricked into participating in an adulterous act (considered a crime) could place her hands on her head symbolizing that she had been forced or coerced into the act. And this public gesture, if enacted as soon as she left the house where the crime occurred, would clear her of any fault.[9] So Tamar may have been signaling her innocence in this act. Likely, she was indicating how she had been degraded and violated, *powerless* to overcome her opponent. Through these gestures she is showing that she has essentially lost everything, and that her very life has been snatched from her. She had been completely overcome with no real way

---

9 Frymer-Kensky, Ibid,165.

of fighting back. Destitute. Powerless. Nearly destroyed.

Furthermore, Tamar refuses to be quiet about what has happened. The text says that "she went away, weeping aloud as she went." Her grief is apparent, evident to everyone. No one had the convenience of ignoring it because she was screaming at the top of her lungs. Her grief poured out like flooding rain. She was hurt, broken, and her public mourning made sure everyone knew it. Tamar had used her voice twice before in this story to protest the assault, but she had been unsuccessful. But this time her voice, her cries of pain reach all who could hear, with each cadence expressing the real depth and weight of her sorrows. And in doing so, she opens the door for the possibility of her own healing.

For this reason, Tamar teaches us the importance of being transparent and honest about our pain. Have you ever known people that refuse to be honest about their feelings? After something horrible happens, you call and check on them. Maybe you stop by to see them. You ask, "Are you all right?" Or "How are you?" The reply is a quick, "Oh, I'm fine." Then they quickly and skillfully change the subject. And you know that nothing could be further from the truth! You can tell they are fighting back tears as they quickly change the subject to get the focus off of them and on to something else. Is this you? Do you have a hard time showing that you're hurt? Do you go out of your way to avoid questions about painful experiences in your life? Do you have a hard time even admitting to yourself when someone has hurt you? Rest assured that is very common. You are not alone. However, let's consider a better way.

In the last chapter we talked about the importance of acceptance, which precedes transparency. We discovered that the first step towards healing from heartache is acknowledging that you've been hurt. That simply means that you must recognize that some bad event has actually happened, which caused you some pain. We also discovered the dangers of denial and refusing to acknowledge what happened. Your pain will continue. Left unchecked it can cause you physical and mental stress and illness, or even evolve into bitterness, rage, and violence. However, when you tell the truth about the painful event in your life, you've taken the first step in dealing with your pain. At that point, healing is possible.

However, if you want to move beyond mere acceptance in the healing process, you must also practice transparency. For some people, accepting what happened is not hard to do. They can easily say, "yes, my boyfriend cheated on me," and take action to end the relationship so that they can move on. Some people are great at telling the truth when someone has done them wrong. They won't hide the fact that the marriage ended. They may even acknowledge that they were hurt by what happened, but they will not be honest about the ongoing pain and loss they feel in their hearts.

When we talk about honesty, we are not merely referring to being honest about the event; that is acceptance. Here, we find Tamar to be so helpful in distinguishing between acceptance and honesty. Notice that after the rape, Tamar accepted what happened. She did not hide, ignore, or try to rewrite or re-imagine the events. She was raped. This thing had happened and it hurt. However, she also cried aloud. In her crying she made it plain to everyone around that she was hurt by the rape. Her public grief demonstrated her own honesty about her pain. Being honest and transparent is about acknowledging your continual pain, grief, and devastation.

When she tore her robe, placed ashes on her head and began to cry aloud, she was being honest with herself about what happened, thereby forcing everyone else to be honest about what happened. And when we can be transparent enough to show our family, friends, and community that we are hurt, then we also open ourselves to ways in which our community can align itself to be of some help to us. Tamar's other brother Absalom heard Tamar's cry and pain, took her into his home, and eventually avenged her rape.[10] Our community of loved ones holds rich resources they can share to aid in our healing. However, the community is incapable of providing help to us when it is not aware of our pain. This is why being transparent about the hurt we feel can ultimately be beneficial to us. If others don't do anything but whisper a prayer for us, it has done us good.

When Jamaal broke up with me, I did not hide my

---

10 Scholars disagree in their interpretation of Absalom's response. While Frymer-Kensky and Birch find him to be cold and self-interested. Trible finds him to be compassionate.

pain from my family and friends, or anyone around me, not even my co-workers. So the very next day, I went to work. Although I do have a great poker face that can be handy at times, that day I left it at home. While I did not want a lot of attention, I certainly did not try to hide my pain. My plan was to keep to myself as much as possible and keep my greetings very brief, but I knew that I would not be able to avoid everyone.

For much of the day I was successful in avoiding people. I made it to my desk without seeing anyone. So I sat down and began to work. I cried off and on all morning. I could not help the heaviness I felt in my chest, so I just let the tears roll down my face throughout the day as I tried to work. I must admit, though, that it was certainly not my most productive day, but I'd rather be there than home alone and crying.

About mid-morning one of my buddies came over to my desk to share a funny story with me. In no mood to joke, I looked up at her and said, "Marian, I'm not having a good day." I hoped that my words would let her know that I did not want to joke around, but as they left my mouth, I watched her face fill with concern. She looked down at me with tears on my cheeks and puffy red eyes and said, "What's wrong?" The look of concern in her eyes and worry in her voice assured me that she really cared, and for that I was grateful. As tears gushed down my face, I shook my head and said, "I don't want to talk about it." She reached out to give me a hug. I stood up and we embraced. I put my head on her shoulder and cried some more. I sat back down and she left. But I knew that she genuinely cared about me and would begin praying as well.

This leads us to another truth about healing: it really is a communal process. You do not have the resources to make it through a painful experience on your own. No one does. So when you turn inward and refuse to talk about your hurt and share openly with others about your pain, you also refuse any help those around you may have to share. You never know what similar painful experiences others have had. They may have advice to share or a resource to offer. Even if they don't, sometimes their presence and concern make you feel better. You know you're not totally alone. Somehow their presence and love give you hope that things will get better. So transparency with loved ones is a critical part of healing because it can lead you to the tools and resources for healing that you would not otherwise have. People who really love you, do want to help you. But they can have no part in a healing process if they don't even know that you need it. You may be thinking, *"Is that it? Just be all open and show all my emotion? Let my heart be seen by loved ones, and I'll feel better?* Well, not exactly. There's a bit more to this.

Reenter Tamar.

We've already noted that when Tamar began weeping aloud as she walked down the street, banished from her brother-rapist's house, discarded like garbage, her cries got the attention of her community; however, the original Hebrew word here for "cry" (za'aq) signifies more. In her weeping (za'aq), Tamar was reaching for God. This powerful God of Israel always hears the cries of the oppressed.[11] It is in this way that Tamar beautifully models lament, reminding us that it is appropriate and best that we begin to process our hurts. In fact, who better to direct them towards than God?

Tamar leads us in the act of being completely transparent, with ourselves, our community, and with God. She cries out to God, and demonstrates her grief publicly. But if she is our model, then how do we imitate her? Are we to put ashes on our heads, rip our clothes, place our hands atop our heads, and scream in the streets? Ummm...Probably not, but there's one incredible resource available to those of us in the deepest of pain, stuck in the most difficult of times—the psalms of lament. They are our tool of release, restoration, and most importantly, prayer.

Have you ever lamented to God, cried out to get God's attention? Even now, as you are perhaps standing in the midst of a heartbreak, have you opened your mouth and let the pain loose and the tears flow? Have you cried out for God in your darkest moments? Perhaps you wanted to, but felt guilty. You've been taught never to question God, rather just trust that somehow God's gonna' "work it out" and everything will "be all right."

---

11 Fremyer-Kensky, Ibid. 166.

But what about when God is silent? What about those moments when you really cannot understand why God allowed this painful experience? What about when you want to critique the action or inaction of the Almighty? We will see, that this lamenting, this wailing of the soul, this desperate cry out to God for relief, this complaint is in fact welcomed by God. It is the way of healing. It is prayer.[12]

Lament, which literally means "to cry," is one of our most powerful tools when walking through the ruins of our life after some tragic event. It gives us a way to express the raw and unedited complaints about the dire circumstances of our lives. Laments are unapologetic and brutally honest utterances of our deepest woes and fiercest pains. They arise from within us during the ugly seasons of life, those moments when the world drastically changes faces before our eyes. Life is unstable, scary, painful, and disorienting. We don't know if we're up or down. The ground collapses underneath us. We are lost, grieving, and unsure. We're in turmoil, pain, confusion, doubt, or other forms of suffering. The person of faith, pushed to the very limits of his or her humanity, cries out to God in utter frustration. Crying, weeping, screaming, lamenting, we are desperate for relief.

Perhaps you lost your job. Your marriage failed. Your child died. A friend committed suicide. Your lover abandoned you. Your best friend betrayed you. Laments

12 Brueggemann, Walter. *Praying The Psalms.* 2nd ed. Eugene, Oregon: Cascade Books, 2007, Kindle, location 286.

grow from these lonely, dark, wilderness experiences when life is anything but pleasant, simple, routine, comfortable, or calm. In fact, the order of life has been totally interrupted, and we are forced into a place of chaos, not sure what our next move should be.[13] Not sure how to act in this confusing, seemingly never-ending season, like Tamar, we don't understand how this was even possible. Completely stunned at what has occurred, we are shaken to the very core by the pain of it all. Even more difficult to fathom is the fact that often things never do return to what they were like before—ever. Life is forever different and there is no going back. Tamar would never be a virgin princess again. So she walks down the street and screams! We don't know what she was saying, but we do know that she wept aloud, making audible the pain in her belly—a pain too heavy and boisterous to keep inside. It's in this most desolate of places that we cry out, with groans so low only God can hear them. And somehow this sad song becomes a routine exercise, carrying us through the most challenging of days.

So what does the lament consist of exactly? Three things, really. First, a lament arises in the context of life's chaos and disorder. Second, it is completely honest. Third, it takes all the awful, uncomely stuff of life directly to God. If you have ever found a way to do those three things, then you have lamented. The lamenter is asking clear questions. Having been stripped of everything familiar and hit with powerful blows, he or she

---

13 *Ibid*, 8-9.

doesn't have much to fear.

"They (lament psalms) are not religious in the sense that they are courteous or polite or deferential. They are religious only in the sense that they are willing to articulate this chaos to the very face of the Holy One." [14]

"The Psalms are an assurance to us that when we pray and worship, we are not expected to censure or deny the deepness of our own human pilgrimage. Rather we are expected to submit it opening and trusting so that it can be brought into eloquent passionate speech addressed to the Holy One." [15]

Walter Brueggeman also discusses the vengeance psalms and his thoughts are helpful here. The vengeance psalms are akin to the lament psalms. They are the really harsh, violent prayers that seek to motivate God to "go after the bad guys." These psalms are full of rage and seek to enlist God to punish, crush, and destroy all those who've done us wrong. These texts appear to be quite antithetical to any faith, as they are far from anything loving and peaceful. We may even secretly wonder why they are in the Bible in the first place. Surely, people of faith should not feel that way. But perhaps sometimes we do. Again, we find the psalms providing an opportunity for expression of our most erratic, violent, painful feelings and desires to God. Rather than acting out our crimes of passion and vengeance, we can leave those

---

14 Brueggemannn, *Ibid*, location 280-286.

15 *Ibid*, location 336.

feelings, hurts and pains before God. [16]

As we walk through the days of our heartbreak, it is certainly normal to feel anger and to want God to do something about it. That raw emotion is real and you shouldn't deny it and pretend it's not there. If you are enraged, then face up to it. Acknowledge it. (Sound familiar?) You don't have to be ashamed of how you feel. Own it, but be sure you are honest with God about it. If you are pissed off about what happened and how your heart was broken, then you are the most appropriate person to pray these psalms. They are there to give you the words to take to God.

And this is not the time to try to determine whose fault it is. That's not appropriate during the lament. Right now, it's about getting your feelings out, expressing to God what your pain is. It doesn't really matter who did what. The point is to be transparent and totally honest with God about what you're feeling. The point of the lament is to say, "I don't like the way things are!" And not in a bratty way, but in a deeply transparent way. Things

---

16 Pete Miko, "Walter Bruggeman Psalms of Vengeance" (taken from Walter Bruggeman's DVD Lecture on the Psalms. Lecture Two—"Disorientation: Faith In The Depths." Lectures recorded at St. Mark's Anglican Church, Niagara-on-the-Lake, June 12-13, 2009), accessed September 1, 2014, https://www.youtube.com/watch?v=rDfzzJD8lpI. Full lectures available on DVD at http://www.mikoproductions.ca/store.html.

are not right. Everything in the universe feels off and out of whack and it is causing me great pain.

Lamenting can be both a moment, a prayer and a particular expression to God, but it can also be an ongoing disposition or practice. And not everyone around you will make the appropriate response. Even those who truly love you may not know the best way to respond because your pain will make them uncomfortable. I'm a pretty happy person most of the time. I'm usually bubbly, smiling a lot, friendly and I love to laugh, but when Jamaal broke up with me, all of that stopped for a while. The heartache was really heavy and I made no attempts to hide it. After a few weeks, this made my mother very uncomfortable. She was worried to death about me. This, of course, is to be expected since she is my mother. But it was like she kept wanting me to snap out of it. She wanted me to look happier, be happier. But the reality was I was hurt and it was going to take awhile for that change. So I continued to be transparent. I did not hide my feelings. I certainly was not putting on a show, but I was simply honest at every moment about how I felt. Your lament will make others uncomfortable, but don't worry about that. You keep on lamenting. Let it out. And take your time. Don't be in a rush. Keep crying out to God until you are done. God won't tire of listening to you.

The lament is critical because it allows us to release all those pent up frustrations. We've already discussed how unhealthy it is to hold all the pain and hurt inside. If we aren't careful, it will do us bodily harm, overwhelm us and/or cause stress, fatigue, illness, or worse. What is beautiful about the lament though is that, in essence, it is a complaint directed toward God. It usually starts by inviting God into the conversation.

THE ELEMENTS OF LAMENT PSALMS

The Invocation.
Get God's attention. Address God however you want. Whichever way you feel comfortable: Loving God, Dear Lord, Father, Mother, YO! Whatever way you are accustomed to calling God's name, do that. Let God know that you want to talk. Rest assured that God is willing to listen.

Complaint
Tell God the problem. What are you upset about? What happened? Was it unfair? Say that! Did it piss you off? Say it! Tell your story. LET. IT. OUT. No filter necessary. Just say it. And don't stop until you've said it. All of it.

Confession of Trust
Affirm your trust in God. This doesn't mean that you like what has happened. It means that you believe God is capable to help, willing to help, present to aid.

Petition
Ask God for what you want, what you think you need. This is usually something like healing, deliverance, relief,

and, in some cases, vengeance. Don't evaluate yourself here. Just share your heart's desire. What things will make you feel better? Whatever it is, just ask.

Vow of Thanksgiving
Promise to praise and thank God, and God only, when your relief comes.

Laments make up nearly one-third of all the Psalms. The Psalmists do us a great service by pouring out their honest complaints so plainly and openly. They show us how to pray in the midst of our most desperate and hopeless moments. Furthermore, there's an entire book in the Old Testament called Lamentations and there are numerous other examples of biblical characters that performed spontaneous laments, pouring out their pain to God. This makes lamenting a biblically and theologically sound practice. It's unfortunate that we don't often hear sermons or preaching about laments, nor are all those troubling texts read in worship services. This is mainly because it makes us uncomfortable to hear those unresolved cries for help and stories of violence and helplessness. The lament Psalms keep it real. They do not sugar coat anything. They tell it like it is. And that raw frankness can be too much for some of us to take. They ask whatever questions they want. They make whatever complaints they want. They accuse whomever they find guilty of causing their pain.

I know all too well the act of lamenting. I recounted

earlier how I screamed at the top of my lungs the night Jamaal and I broke up. I rolled around in my bed, unable to be consoled. I was so loud I disturbed my neighbors, but there was no stopping of the sound. The cries flowed painfully and continuously out of me. And I believe that God received it. I even went so far in my moment of lament to question God. I asked, "Who are you?!?!?!?!" I could not comprehend how it was that I'd gotten back to this place again. Very often people are not comfortable when you raise such daring questions to God. That is because when we critique, question, accuse, and even dare to admonish God, we are challenging most people's basic theological assumptions: That God is all powerful and cannot be questioned. Some might even accuse you of having no faith.

I believe that God actually welcomes the lament openly as a valid form of prayer. What God desires most from us human beings is an honest and intimate relationship. So when Tamar pours out her pain, I think she is hoping to get God's attention, to communicate with God and, perhaps, be in dialogue with God about the depths of her sorrows. This is relationship. And I've always held that even if that relationship is occasionally strained, it is still a relationship.

Finally, take note that lament is rooted in hope. While it might seem like I'm encouraging you to go on and on, whining, and crying about things you can't change, that's not really the goal here. We only lament because we believe better is possible. We lament because we refuse to accept life as it is. In fact, the only reason we even say anything to God is because we have witnessed what God has done in the past. We have seen God transform someone's prison into a paradise. We've seen God bring new life out of death. We've seen God's resurrecting power completely turn things around. So the lamenter is actually a person of incredible faith because he or she still hopes in the midst of the most dismal of circumstances. They believe beyond the moment. There is hope in the holler.[17]

This is not meaningless weeping, but the cry itself is an act of faith, a conviction that a new order is being established, that new life will break through the dead reality of the suffering. In that sense, the lament leads us to praise. Some of us want to immediately jump to the praise when tragedy hits, to prove we're faithful or committed or truly sold out for God, but it's so important to walk *through* the "valley of the shadow of death," and all its ominous dwellings. For here our faith is developed and strengthened in ways not possible elsewhere. It is in that dark valley that we meet a powerful and compassionate God who journeys with us.

So as you have considered the concept of being transparent in your pain, how might the lament help you through the dark hour of your heartbreak? How can you make lament your practice? And please note that

17 This phrase is borrowed from A. Elaine Brown Crawford's text, *Hope In The Holler: A Womanist Theology.* Westminster John Knox Press: Louisville, 2002.

laments can be as creative as they need to be. People of various cultures have found ways to lament: poetry, singing, the blues, and art. There are so many ways to approach this. But the question is what are you feeling? What is the pain you are carrying? Anger? Loss? Humiliation? Have you felt violated like Tamar? Did you feel rejected like me? What is your pain? What is your story? It's time for you to really engage it. I want you to write, sing, pray, dance, your own lament. If you were responsible for writing the 151st Psalm, what would your psalm sound like?

Using the elements of lament we discussed above, please write your own lament in the space provided. Take your time. The rules? Be honest. Address the Holy. Don't censure yourself. Be raw. Be direct.

INVOCATION GET GOD'S ATTENTION...

COMPLAINT WHAT ARE YOU UPSET ABOUT? HOW DID IT FEEL? WHAT HAPPENED? WHO DID IT? HOW DID IT AFFECT YOU?

CONFESSION OF TRUST TELL GOD THAT YOU HAVE FAITH IN GOD'S CHARACTER.

PETITION WHAT DO YOU WANT GOD TO DO ABOUT IT? WHAT DO YOU WANT FROM GOD?

THANKSGIVING WHAT CAN YOU GIVE GOD THANKS FOR?

REFLECTIONS HOW DID YOU FEEL IN THIS PROCESS? WHAT DID YOU LEARN?

When we find ourselves in these unsettling times of life, feeling scared, bewildered, and worried sick about where to go and how things will turn out for us, we usually find a way to talk about it. We discuss it with friends, family. Perhaps some of us resort to typing those lengthy and perhaps too-revealing status updates on Facebook to get our feelings out. Others might go on Twitter rants, which I don't usually advise. The point is we find a way to get stuff off our chests. However, the lament is a much healthier option because it allows us to process our pain theologically, directing our complaints to God. This is a much more fruitful and productive way of releasing our pain. God is a safe space to release the ugliest of our thoughts and the weightiest of our worries without judgment, or possibility of hurting ourselves or others in the process.

We are indebted to the lament psalmists because they take teach us how to take the most difficult, hopeless, painful experiences of our lives and address the Holy One. They really teach us to pray our way through the pain, leaving our woes with the one who can comfort, console, love, guide, and heal us.

"It won't be like this always. There'll be better days."
—Jessica Reedy on "Always" from "From The Heart"

CHAPTER SIX PRACTICING QUIET INVITING GOD INTO YOUR BROKENNESS

"Come, behold the works of the Lord; see what desolations he has brought on the earth. He makes wars to cease to the end of the earth...
Be still and know that I am God..."
Psalm 46:8-9a, 10a

Be still.
Get quiet.
Settle down.
Find calm.
Listen.
Breathe.
Breathe again.

Rest

Wait.

Heal.

These are some of the last things you might want to do while in the midst of a horrible heartbreak. In fact, your mind is probably the opposite of anything calm or quiet. Your world is likely loud and boisterous, rocky, and as monstrous as a thunderstorm that it seems ridiculous for anyone to *dare* suggest you be... *quiet?* But the Lord calls out to us in the midst of the chaos to simply be still. While you may want to run, scream, cry, shout, make a call, ambush or confront someone, throw a temper tantrum, start a fight, take action, *do something*, (ANYTHING!) in order to change things, fix things, and rid yourself of the pain, I've found that the best thing to do if you want to heal is to practice stillness and quietness. The silence itself is a haven for healing, a refuge in the arms of God.

Let me explain.

CUT THE CHATTER

Practicing quiet helps to insulate you from the drama that results from constantly talking about your heartbreak. When we feel we've been wronged, it's very natural to want to call up our girlfriend, your mama, auntie, big cousin, or whoever will listen to us pour out our pain, co-sign on our outrage, and be ready to fight and act a fool with us. While it is absolutely vital that you talk to *someone* when you're going through a tough time, you should not talk to everyone or too much! This is not helpful to you at all.

It's like pouring salt on an open wound. It stings!

The more you tell and retell the story of your heartbreak *before you've healed*, the more you rehearse and relive your pain. It's like you can't begin to heal because you're frozen in time. You can't move forward because you're totally preoccupied with the past. This is self-defeating, unfruitful activity. Don't do it.

In contrast, creating some quiet and calm in your life will help shield you from additional trauma. The pain you feel is very real. I get it. It won't go away immediately, and, no, the quiet won't force it right out. But if you aren't careful about how, when, and with whom you talk about your experience, you will keep opening yourself up for more hurt. While your friends and loved ones may mean you well, all of them aren't always capable of providing you with the best advice. They want to, but they may not be equipped to do so.

You have no idea what unhealed hurts and pains people are carrying around, and sometimes even they aren't aware of them. So when they open their mouths to help you, they aren't giving you the most clear, substantive, well thought-out, well-tested advice. Rather they are actually working to make sense of their own unresolved pain under the *guise* of "helping you." But because you are broken and hurt, desperate for any words that will encourage you or provide some relief, you trust their words, perhaps blindly, and have now taken in all their stuff—pain, confusion, distrust, fear, resentment, etc. You've now consumed everything you don't need without even realizing it all because it sounded like good, solid, helpful advice from someone who loves you.

Other times, people do really have wonderful things to say to you and great advice to give. They've been where you are and they made it through the heartbreak. They know the mountains you must climb and the valleys you're going to have to cross. More importantly, they have saved the map and believe they can tell you exactly how to maneuver through the terrain of your pain. Yet, you have to pace yourself, and receive their guidance when you're ready.

I remember just a few days after Jamaal and I broke up, I received some premature advice. It was late one night, and I was pulling into a parking spot across from my apartment. It had been another long day of carrying the weight of this new heartbreak around, and really I just wanted to crawl into my bed as fast as I could and try to sleep. As I put the car in park, I saw my phone light up. Realizing it was a text message, I quickly picked up the phone and when I saw the name, fear shot through my chest. It was from one of my mentors, a person whom I love very much and whose wisdom has guided me at many critical moments in my life. But in this instance I had a feeling that it was going to be something I was not ready to hear just yet. Something[18] told me not to read it, but the curiosity got to me and I opened the message.

He was not the final prize. He was just a glimpse.

---

18 I'm sure this was God's Spirit whispering to me.

Ouch!!! That stung me so hard. I realize that this was meant to encourage me, to help me to consider that there was something better out there, that this whole experience with Jamaal was just a prequel to a much more wonderful adventure in love that was to come. However, I couldn't see that far into the future and those words could not comfort me then. I was still holding on to the past, at least in my heart. At that moment I was barely keeping my head above the painful waters of heartbreak, trying my best to keep from drowning. I was working really hard at accepting what had happened, but I still daydreamed about Jamaal and I reconciling. I fantasized about him calling me back and telling me he'd made a mistake. And honestly, that was a comforting thought. It was nothing I was going to act on, but it sometimes made me feel better. So the words in that message came across so abruptly, and were frankly uninvited. We hadn't even been chatting that day, so the text just came out of nowhere; I wasn't expecting it. And the message of it was so final: it was a blatant reminder that my fantasies were just that—fantasy. Now to this person's credit, I know this message was sent in love and actually it was the truth! But it was a truth I was not quite ready to hear in my heart. I needed more time and I needed to do a lot more healing before I could dream about a better love.

In extreme cases, people can be flat out pushy and try to move you too fast. They mean well, but they want you to take the step now. Act now! Understand and feel better now! And they will often give the *right* advice at the *wrong* time—way too soon! They are excited about the victory that awaits you and can be less than patient about your getting there. They don't mean to rush you, but they so want you to get to the healing part that they forget about the process. It takes time. And your process *will be* different from theirs. Not everyone can appreciate those differences. Moreover, no two healing processes are the same; healing plays out differently for everyone. Let's consider a couple of biblical examples.

The Gospel of John (5:1-9) tells the story of a man who was ill and who lived in Jerusalem and laid at Sheep Gate. There were five porches there where many people who were sick would lay. The text says this particular man had been sick for 38 years. Can you imagine? 38 years! Day after day, week after week, year after year, he was just lying there sick with no prospects for healing and no real hope for relief. Jesus saw him lying there and approached him, asking, "Do you want to be healed?" The man explains that when the angel comes to trouble the water, he has no one to help him into the pool and someone always gets in ahead of him, beating him to the miracle of healing. Jesus' responds, "Stand up, take up your mat, and walk." The text says that, "at once the man was made well..."

In his Gospel, Mark tells a very different healing story (5:24-34) of a woman who had been hemorrhaging for twelve years. The writer says that she has spent all of her money going to different doctors, but none of them had been able to help. In fact, her condition was getting worse, but she had heard about Jesus and how we was healing people. Not wanting to make herself known, when she saw him passing through her town, she pushed through the crowd resolved that if she could just touch his garment, she would be healed of her disease. Mark says that she was right, because upon touching Jesus' garment, she was healed immediately. Jesus, recognizing that healing power had gone out of him, wanted to know who touched him. When she identified herself, he said to her, "Daughter, your faith has made you well; go in peace and be healed of your disease."

Let's consider the similarities and the differences in the two stories. In both cases, there is a person who has been sick for a long time and is in need of healing. One was female and the other male. While the woman has been sick twelve years, the man has been ill more than three times as long as she. The woman's problem is incurable hemorrhaging, but the man's ailment is never actually named. While the text indicates that the woman has exhausted all of her financial resources seeking relief from her problem, it doesn't seem the man has done much of anything to resolve his physical challenge. In fact, it suggests that he has no resources, not even a person who would help him in the pool. Further, he looks to be healed by a miracle which he believes will occur in the pool, while she has sought help from physicians for her healing. He has a conversation with Jesus about his predicament, whereas she doesn't even want to be seen by Jesus, much less talk to him. They are two very different people, with different kinds of problems, two different ideas on how to fix their problems, and different stories and experiences of pain altogether.

The biggest difference I see between the two hurting people, though, is that the woman sees Jesus and goes after her own healing, while the man does not. In contrast, Jesus sees him and goes to him to initiate his healing process. I love that the Bible provides both these stories of healing because it shows the diversity of ways in which healing takes place. For some of us, we chase God down to get what we need, others of us feel helpless to do anything to change our situation. In either instance, I find God to be incredibly merciful, in that God looks at each of us with compassion and love, desiring that each of us be healed and restored, and provides a remedy that will work *for us*. We are not all the same, and our healing experiences won't be the same either. So never feel like you have to take the exact steps someone else took to get past the pain.

That's why in this book, I want to emphasize certain *practices* that lead to healing (acceptance, honesty, and quiet). It's about thinking in ways and making choices that are life-giving, but it's certainly not some one-size-fits-all easy 1-2-3 formula. I do not think that everyone should do the exact same things I did to be healed. The truth is: you and I are two different people. We've loved different people. We've experienced different things. Our heartbreaks transpired in totally different circumstances. Why in the world would the story of our healing play out the same? They won't. And I won't pretend I know exactly how your story will end, but I do know there are practices, ways of being, and choices that you can make that lead to healing.

One of those choices, is quieting yourself and your world down, and using discernment about who and how often you talk about what happened. Be careful about who you allow to speak into your life. There are some people with whom you simply will not be able to discuss your pain because they just aren't helpful. They don't have a pastoral bone in their body, and have no idea how to talk to you while you're in such a delicate state. You will have to throw up the deuces and catch up with them when you're feeling better. You only need prayers, support, and positivity at first—not some well-meaning friend's harsh and unsolicited advice. While they may be telling you the truth, it may be way too soon for you to hear it. And anytime someone starts out with this line, "You may not want to hear this right now, but..." beware. Something that hurts is almost sure to follow. You don't need that now. It's all just too much! Too many opinions! Too much noise! TOO MUCH! You need to rest your heart, not get it all worked up again. Quietness will give your heart a break, providing you a refuge from the noise of your pain.

Now let's be clear, I'm not encouraging you to keep everything bottled up either. It *is* important to get things off your chest. We have already discussed practicing honesty as very important to the healing process. So of course, you should tell close friends and family what happened. This helps you acknowledge it. You don't want to pretend it didn't happen, hiding from family and friends, avoiding the truth. But you also do not want to take up permanent residence in your painful story because you are constantly talking about it. It happened. It hurt. It probably still hurts. It sucked and it will continue to suck for awhile, but you are not required to meditate on it day and night through rehashing the story. This is not helpful to you or anyone around you. Have you ever told a story and found yourself getting madder than you were? That's what rehashing your hurt can do; make you more hurt than you were before. So be careful how much you retell the story and to whom.

Another way to think of it is to recall a time you skinned your knee playing as a child (if you weren't the playful active type, just go with me here). After you came limping home with that bloody awful knee, your mom or dad probably cleaned it with water, alcohol, or peroxide, rubbed some Neosporin on it, threw on a band-aid, and told you to "leave it alone." And if you were obedient, in a few short days, your scar healed up all the way. But if you played with the Band-Aid, picked at the scar, you know, did everything but "leave it alone," I guarantee it took longer to heal. There is something about space, quiet, and time that allow healing to take place, but if you keep rehashing and stirring in your pain, then that is what you will constantly feel and where you will constantly stay.

So how is this possible? How can you be both

transparent and quiet at the same time? Well, for me that meant only discussing my situation with a *select few* people, but not often. Rather than constantly talking about my pain and reliving the story over and over, I alerted people in my support system to pray for me. And I made time to pray for myself. I intentionally spent more time at home during those days and when I was there, I shut the world out. I wasn't spending hours on social media or talking on the phone. I would literally sit in silence and pray. I took slow deep breaths and sat quietly and listened intently for God's voice. That solace was comforting to me. It gave my mind and heart a break from trying to fix it, change it, or figure it out. It was restful, restorative, and soothing.

At the same time, when I was around other people, I did not go out of my way to pretend I was feeling good all the time. Most of the time I didn't feel good. And if people noticed, well then they just noticed. I made no attempts to dress up or cover up my pain. That would've required more energy than I had to give. I know that the change in my disposition to a more sad tone probably made a few loved ones uncomfortable, but oh well. Hopefully that prompted them to pray for me, something I desperately needed them to do anyway. While I was not trying to draw attention to myself, I simply practiced being honest about how (bad) I felt at every moment. I allowed whatever negative or painful feelings which came up to the surface, to come out and be expressed honestly and released. There was no suppressing, no masking, no faking.

As I shared earlier, the morning after Jamaal and I broke up, I sent this text message to my inner circle:

Last night, Jamaal told me he had no romantic feelings for me. We broke up. I am devastated. I don't want to talk about it. Please just pray.

Right at the beginning I did three things: First, I acknowledged what happened, "We broke up," (acceptance). I was transparent in my hurt, "I'm devastated" (honesty). Finally, I asked for space, "I don't want to talk," (quietness) while still inviting the love and support from my loved ones—*in the way I needed it*—by asking for their prayers.

It's like a scene from the 2008 remake of the film, The Women—one of my favs! Mary Haines' (Meg Ryan) three best friends (Annette Bening, Debra Messing, and Jada Pinkett Smith) work themselves up into a frenzy when they find out Mary's husband is having an affair. Wanting to help her, they plan an intervention of sorts in order to tell Mary the horrible news. Much to their surprise Mary tells them she already knew about the affair and admitted that she hadn't confronted her husband yet. Her friends are appalled at the passive role she's assumed in all this and start telling her she must to do something about it, stand up for herself! They love her and know that she deserves so much better! So rather than listening and caring for Mary and her needs in the moment, before long all the women are arguing with each other about how Mary should proceed. Fed up, Mary finally says,

"Okay, okay! Alright! I appreciate all of you trying to help. I really do, but please don't dissect and analyze every square inch of this right now; I can't take it! Just *be there* for me...SILENTLY!"

I love it! Clear. Honest. Direct. Sometimes you just have to tell people what you need from them, refusing to accept anything else.

It's natural for our loved ones to want to help us, but we have to tell them the best ways *to* help. It may or may not be a long conversation every day. It may be a hug, a smile, space, or simply a prayer. Do talk to your loved ones. Tell them what happened. Tell someone how you feel, but also tell them *how* to help you. Have them help you to create an environment of healing in your life. And know that you will need to constantly assess your own needs. What you need from them today might be different from what you need tomorrow. Pay attention to yourself and how you're feeling and make decisions that will keep moving you forward.

"In returning and rest shall ye be saved, in quietness and in confidence
shall be your strength..."
Isaiah 30:15

One benefit of creating quiet in your life, is finding clarity. I remember when I first started seeing my spiritual director, Diana.[19] It happened to be during the aftermath of Mike. I had accepted his decision, but it still hurt. And I was slowly trying to make my way through the thick of it. Somewhere in the midst of all that Diana advised me to start taking 5 to 10 minutes of quiet each day; this would be my devotional practice. During this time I was not supposed to read scripture, sing, pray, write, or anything. I was literally supposed to sit in absolute silence (no TV, phone, ipod, or internet) as my way of spending time with God. My only instruction was to "be still and know that I am God (Psalm 46:10)." And this would be my discipline every single day.

Well, surprisingly, nothing interesting happened during those quiet moments. There was no outpouring of God's spirit. No tears, no, magic, nothing particularly exciting happened at all during my quiet time. Each day my devotion was just as uneventful as the devotion the day before it. This was my first time trying such a thing. I'd always thought devotion required at least some scripture reading. After a few weeks, I'd begun to worry that

---

19 Spiritual Direction is a meeting between a Spiritual Director, aka, a trained listener, and a person who is seeking more in her (or his) life. It is an opportunity to share one's story and gain God's perspective on one's journey. For more information on "spiritual direction," please see the resources section in the back of the book.

nothing was happening so I mentioned it to Diana. She told me not to worry about that, but to continue my discipline so I did. Each morning before leaving for work, I sat in absolute silence for at least 10 minutes.

Then one evening, I was driving home from work. I think the radio played in the background, but I was quiet and not really listening. As I accelerated and braked along Interstate 70, heading east with a thousand of other motorists, all of a sudden Mike and that whole situation came to mind: him, the baby, the mother, my hurt and disappointment, all of it. And out of nowhere I heard, "I don't really want all that in my life right now." There it was. The truth I'd been too hurt to notice before then. Suddenly, I understood that I simply wasn't ready to date Mike anyway. Though I'd previously said I was willing to, the truth was that's not what I wanted. Yes, I wanted Mike, but I didn't want the whole child with another woman baggage. The thought of dating someone in that situation, apparently really overwhelmed me and it was more than I cared to have going on in my life. Up until that point, I had no idea that I even felt that way. It was buried somewhere beneath all my hurt feelings.

I cannot tell you how that realization comforted me. For months, I carried the hurt of having been rejected by Mike. I was deeply saddened by the potential love and relationship I thought I had lost. And all the while, underneath it all I simply wasn't ready to deal with everything he brought to the table. Though my feelings for him prompted me to fight for him (at least in my head) and constantly fantasize about ways we could "figure it out," deep down inside, I apparently didn't want any of it. Talk about a revelation. It felt so good to finally relax about what I thought I had lost. It was a huge a relief. I was freed from the worry and some of the pain.

And more interesting than that? This truth emerged from the depths of me, not from some long session of analyzing the situation with my best friend. It didn't come out of a tearful heart-to-heart with my mom. It did not even come to me after hearing some phenomenal sermon. No, it emerged from the quietness I'd been practicing. Deep inside I heard God's still small voice. It affirmed that this wasn't what I really wanted anyway. After discussing this with Diana, I saw that this was God's response to my discipline of quiet. So although nothing spectacular happened during the quiet time, something incredibly reassuring and powerful grew from it. Because I had disciplined my spirit to be quiet and still, I could hear the voice of God speak softly inside, pointing me to the truth I'd desperately needed.

And let me be clear. Yes, I did hear the words, "I don't want this," and not "You don't want this." So you may ask, "How do you know that was God speaking to you? Weren't you just hearing your own voice?" And I wouldn't disagree with you there, but it was God who was quietly nudging me, making my own truth clearer than it had ever been. Now I knew how to move forward. And in that moment I took a giant step forward in my healing.

QUIETNESS AS SPACE

There's another layer of understanding quietness that we must explore here. It's not only about cutting down the noise, but it's also about creating space. It's about giving yourself room to breathe, getting some air. It's about creating some distance between you and the situation, you and the person, you and your heartbreak, or a combination of these—whatever your particular need is. Quietness as space involves creating both physical and psychological distance from the source of your heartbreak. "Psychological distance?" Are you thinking, "Girl what are you talking about?" LOL. Let's talk about it.

Physical distance

It can be really difficult to heal when you have to constantly look in the face of the person who broke your heart. Every time you see them, hear their voice, that pain shoots right up through your body, your heart, up your throat and sometimes right out of your mouth. This is natural, painful, and causes a lot of wear and tear on your heart. So if it is not absolutely necessary that you see or talk to this person, then don't. One thing I know helped me to heal was not being around Jamaal after we broke up. He had the grand idea that we should remain friends. Keep in mind, that although he said he had no more romantic feelings for me, he said he still really liked me as a person. He'd even told me, "You're the most amazing woman I've ever met," so he had every hope that we could still talk and hang out. You know... be friends; but when he suggested we maintain a friendship, I was like, "No thanks. I have friends." While that might sound really harsh or perhaps even cold, I was completely serious.

I knew that at that time being Jamaal's friend was far beyond what I could reasonably do. There was no way I was going to be able to fill that role. Here's why: Jamaal was completely over his romantic feelings for me, but I still had those feelings for him. His feelings had changed, but mine had not. He'd already had the privilege of adjusting to the change, but I was only now learning about it. He'd taken time to think about how he felt and had already accepted that the relationship was over, allowing him to begin making the necessary emotional adjustments while I was just starting to process it all. The person who initiates the break-up is usually a bit further along in the recovery process than the person on the receiving end. Jamaal had the inside track on the breakup. He had the heads up. On the contrary, I had no idea any of this was coming.

This breakup business was all very new and fresh for me; I still had girlfriend feelings and desires for him and I could not pretend they weren't there. In those set of circumstances, a "friendship" would've only served to confuse and hurt me further. This is where we see how space and acceptance go hand in hand. By keeping my distance from Jamaal, it helped to reinforce in my mind that the relationship was, in fact, over. So the space helped ensure I really accepted what had happened. On the flip, because I had accepted it, I kept my distance from him.

Now if I had interrupted that flow by still being around him as his "friend," this would have made it hard for me to accept that it was really over. This would have no doubt aroused my feelings for him all over again, and made me excited about being around him. It would've given me hope, though false and baseless, but hope, nonetheless, that we would get back together. In reality, Jamaal had already stated that he was no longer interested in being with me so getting back together wasn't going to happen. And whenever I would've come to realize that "no" he doesn't really want to be with me and really only wants to be "friends," I would've been hurt all over again. If I had promised to be his friend, I may still have felt like I had to force myself to somehow maintain a friendship despite the emotional strain it was causing me. Thus the cycle would start over again. Do you see the back and forth here? It's quite a violent exercise to put your heart through over and over again just for the sake of being someone's "friend." Truthfully, real friendships don't feel like that at all. They don't cause constant strain and pain on top of pain. And who would I have to blame for allowing this less-than-a-friendship—and all the stress that comes with it—into my space? Nobody but myself. And I was simply not willing to play that game with my heart. Ultimately, this kind of environment just isn't conducive to healing.

Even if I wanted to be friends with Jamaal, I simply wasn't capable of it. Emotionally speaking, I was not ready to make such an abrupt switch. And anyway, when people say they still want to be your "friend," what they usually mean is that they still would like to have you around as an option. Or they don't want you to hate them. In my opinion, if both people aren't ready for the breakup and in an emotionally good place, a friendship just isn't feasible.

More than that, I knew that I needed space to process what I was feeling, to examine what happened. To heal. I was in no condition to be his friend. What I needed more than anything was space, air, and room to breathe. And I did not need him all up in that space, clogging it up, sucking up my oxygen, confusing me, and slowing down my healing process. If the relationship was over, I just needed to accept that and get focused on healing my heart—and I simply did not need him around to do that. He would have been the worst possible distraction at the time. He had to go.

For the record, I did not hate Jamaal. He certainly was not my favorite person at the time, but at least I could say he was honest. Though I think he could've given me a warning or prepared me a little better, but how well can you really be prepared for a breakup? Either way, I was headed for heartbreak. And if the hurt was inevitable, it was critical that I immediately start making choices that would allow for my healing. I had to make myself the priority. In my case, that meant I had to choose not to be his friend.

If you want to heal from your hurt, you've got to learn how to care for yourself during the process. That's what we want to focus on here. What are the decisions you need to make for you, which would create a peaceful and safe space for you to heal? What does that world look like? Imagine it. Who is present? Who is not? Who is going to help you move forward? Make choices that serve *you* best. Make self-care a high priority. Be selfish for once! Do not create a world for yourself that is so full of pain and confusion that you literally suffocate in it. You need quiet and clarity. This fosters healing. And if that's what you want for yourself, then go after it and let no one get in your way—not even you.

Never forget that there is something better waiting for you on the other side of this pain. There is a life that is joyful and full of peace. It belongs to you, but you have to choose it.

One further caveat here. Now I realize that every heartbreak does not necessarily involve a break-up, but if yours does then please know that you are going to have to shut down any sexual activity with your ex. Please do not lie to yourself and say that "it's just sex" or "I just need some." Believe me, I understand. The breakup may have left you horny as a toad, particularly if you had a pretty active sex life together, and you may miss your lover terribly and all the fire y'all made. However, let me warn you that having sex with this person will only serve to confuse you. Again, this will likely give you false hope that things will change, and they may not. If it's over, then it's over—and sex is not going to change that.

Most importantly, sex will cloud your mental and emotional space—the space you desperately need in order to heal. In that sense, sex is completely counter-productive. How can you think clearly and discern what is the best way to move forward if you're still dwelling in the past? It's no different than constantly talking about what happened or talking to the wrong people. It keeps you imprisoned to your pain, dwelling in the negativity. If it's really over, then you have to make choices that reflect that— that is, if you want to heal. And remember you need *space* to heal, specifically space from the person who hurt you. Sex does nothing but reignite the flames of passion and likely keep you wanting to be with your ex. Though it will certainly serve as a kind of reunion, it won't necessarily rekindle the relationship. Don't trick yourself into thinking you can get over someone if you're still sleeping with them. You can't. You need to remove the person and even some of the things that remind you of him or her from your physical and mental space. Your ex has to go so that you can begin to heal.

Don't think you can play the dating game either; if you're really breaking up, then cut all contact if possible. Start shutting everything down, gradually if you have to: hanging out, sex, phone calls, dating, the "friendship," all of it. Those things are just the various aspects of the relationship—you know, the one that ended. Don't engage any of it. This is a setup for another let down, which will cause you more hurt, more pain—the very things which will complicate and retard the healing process. Sometimes it can be difficult, impossible even, to shut it all off cold turkey; you may have to gradually pull away. I've found that strategy works well for me. The important part is that you do make the effort to really leave, even if it takes awhile to completely cut contact. If there was a breakup, then *break up.*

You may be thinking, *Arionne, girl, this is ridiculous! You are asking way too much. I am not capable of all this!* Listen, I completely feel you. And I do not mean to suggest that any of this is easy, nor to imply that you can achieve it alone. You probably can't. I couldn't. But here is the blessing: if we are *honest* about our own shortcomings and frailties, then we are in the best possible position to receive help from the only one who is capable of helping us navigate through the turbulent waters of a heartbreak anyway—God.

"But he said to me, 'My grace is sufficient for you, for power is made perfect in weakness.' So I will boast all the more gladly of my weaknesses, so that the power of Christ may dwell in me."

—2 Corinthians 12:9

At the end of his second letter to the Corinthians, the Apostle Paul talks about some kind of thorn (or pain) in his flesh which is causing him great discomfort. After praying about this three times, asking God to remove it, the Lord responds assuring Paul that God's grace will suffice for him. When Paul is weak, then God will be strong in him, for God's power is made perfect in our weakness. Paul goes on and concludes...

"Therefore I am content with weaknesses, insults, hardships, persecutions, and calamities for the sake of Christ; for whenever I am weak, then I am strong."
—v. 10

How reassuring for us to learn that we aren't required to be powerful, strong, and capable all the time. In fact, it's in our weak moments that God desires to show God's incredible power through us, enabling us to do far more than we ever thought possible. It is tough to set boundaries for yourself in the midst of a heartbreak. The very thing you want to do is run back to the one you love, right back to the place of your hurt. God knows and understands this, and is willing to help you if you just ask.

Years ago, in my very early twenties, there was this guy who I really liked. He was fine as hell! He was older, a professional, a smooth talker, charmer, sexy, intelligent, well-spoken, wheeeew! He was just everything! The most exciting part was that he was attracted to me too! That blew my mind. I couldn't believe this guy was into me. He lived out of town, though, so we used to talk on the phone, text, and flirt all the time. Our conversations were nothing less than steamy. The chemistry between us was absolutely "electric," as he rightfully described it one day. And I knew that should we ever have the opportunity to get together, there was no telling what might happen.

However, even though I was very attracted to him sexually, I also knew that getting physical with him might not be the best decision. He was older and had years of experience in dating. He had spent a lot of time with women, over the course of his player career, and he had plenty of game, which gave him quite an advantage over me. I was a very young, vulnerable, and naive "tenderoni," just ripe for him to pounce on, but something in me knew that he probably meant me no good. I just sensed that if we got too involved, it would be all bad for me. I am convinced that was the Holy Spirit trying to get my attention and help me make a good decision. (Thank you LORD!) So after some thinking, I resolved that even though it was highly possible that I might sleep with him, I should try my best not to. I also knew the only way I would be successful was if I asked God for help. There was no way I would be able to tell him no on my own. No way!!! Let me repeat: He WAS FINE!!! The attraction was so mutual and the chemistry was way too strong.

Well, the timing was right for such a prayer because the season of Lent was beginning and my church was doing a fast where we were praying and did not eat until noon each day throughout the Lenten season. We were praying for a lot of different things as a congregation, but

I added to my list of petitions a request that God would keep me from sleeping with him. And yes, I was just that frank with God. "Lord, don't let me sleep with him. I know, given the right circumstance, I probably will, but I really don't want to. Please help me not to." [20] This was my sincere and earnest prayer that I prayed every day for 40 days straight. For the most part, keeping to this goal of no sex with him was easy. After all he lived out of town. No big deal, right? Well until...

He called me one day to let me know that he was going to be in town on business that week. He thought we should get together and have dinner. Well the evening was all planned. I had a singing engagement that afternoon and he came through to support me. Originally, he said he wasn't sure he'd make it, but that we'd definitely hang out after. So imagine my thrill when he walked in the door. Well, played, sir. Very well played. This, of course, made my day, had me excited and very open. We left and got in his Hummer (yes, the Hummer), and headed out to dinner. He wasn't leaving until the next morning and it was early. So we had the whole evening to ourselves to do whatever, wherever, however. It was definitely about to be on and cracking! You could probably just about guess how the evening ended, but...

As soon as we pulled off, he started to complain

20 It is my strong conviction that God does desire to hear this level of transparency from us. Nothing is too edgy, blunt, or raw for prayer. I've learned to speak my truth however I need to speak it. God knows anyway.

about his stomach feeling sick. He kept grabbing his waist, trying to drive with one hand. At some point, he just pulled over and sat there for a minute until he felt better. Trying to shake it off, player that he was, he started driving again. Eventually we stopped at a CVS to get him a 7up, but even that did not help. He was sick and nothing was helping. After about 30 minutes, he looked at me and said, "I'm so sorry, but I need to take a rain check on dinner. I'm just not feeling well and I'm afraid I won't be very good company tonight." WHAT? I couldn't believe this happened. Five minutes later, I was back home with nothing else planned for my Friday night. He pulled off and that was that. Yep, God answers prayers.

I later realized that his food poisoning episode served as my protection, my route of escape! That might sound crazy, but imagine it: Everything was set up perfectly. We had the whole rest of the night to do anything we wanted. We were both grown, legal, single, and strongly attracted to each other. There was no one to interrupt, no competing plans. Just us, our desires, and a free night together. The stage was completely set, but he was so sick that he couldn't even drive. It was unreal. So a night of passion was definitely out of the question. Had things gone his way, or our way, that man would have turned me all the way out that night. I would've definitely bit off way more than I could've possibly chewed and who knows how long it would've taken for me to recover. I am convinced that God helped me that day, made sure I didn't sleep with him, simply because I'd asked.

I share this to say that Paul was absolutely right, God's strength is made perfect in our weakness. If you are having trouble breaking your sexual bond with your ex, ask for God to help. God's always willing to help us, no matter what the situation is. When we are honest with ourselves *and with God* about our weaknesses, then we recognize our real need for God who is always happy to help, protect, strengthen, and sustain us. God wants to be part of our story, wants to be our support, be our companion—be whatever we need. We only need to ask. Rest assured when we invite God in, the answer is always yes.

So know that whatever decisions you need to make in order to set the stage for your healing, you are totally capable of making them with God's help. Know that you are not alone in the journey toward your healing, God desires to walk with you, empowering and encouraging you every step of the way. You can do this, not because you are strong, but because God is. You are actually pretty frail, perhaps even discouraged, but God who loves you unconditionally is powerful, able, and willing to lift you up and help you along.

"I lift up my eyes to the hills—from where will my help come? My help comes from the Lord, who made heaven and earth."

Psalm 121:1-2

Beyond physical space...

I've gone on and on about creating physical distance from

the person who broke your heart, but what if that simply isn't possible? What if you have a child with the one who broke your heart? What if you work together? Suppose you live in the same apartment complex? Perhaps you have mutual friends? Perhaps there's a combination of several of these circumstances or some other unique predicament that makes it impossible for you to avoid him/her completely? Does this mean there is no peace for you? Is your healing necessarily harder to achieve, will it take longer to reach, or is it less practical? I say no. While in some instances, it's not exactly possible to be completely away from the person physically, that doesn't have to slow down your healing; you just have to create that space mentally. How, you ask?

First, note that you *can* refrain from certain physical contact in any break-up situation: dating, sex, casual talking, flirting, etc. These are the very things that were part of the relationship and you don't want to confuse yourself by still engaging in them. And look, I know slip ups can and often happen. Don't beat yourself up too much if one does. If at first you don't succeed...well, you know the rest.

Second, keep the focus of the contact with the person on the new nature of your relationship. If you are no longer his woman but still the mother of his child, then keep your interactions focused on the needs and concerns for your child. Be careful not to mix your common bond with the broken relationship. That means don't punish him for breaking up with you by not letting him see his child or creating extra drama in order for him to see the child. Focus on the child, not your broken relationship. If you work together, I certainly wouldn't suggest you quit your job but do keep your relationship professional. Don't use work time to talk about getting back together or lashing out at one another. The transition will be hard enough, don't make the time you have to be around each other unbearable. This will only get your feelings worked up and have you thinking about him/her even when you're not at work.

Keep in mind that the whole goal of limiting your physical contact anyway is to clear your headspace. So if you still have to have contact, then don't do things that will cloud up your mind. Try to keep things as peaceful as possible. Be very intentional about focusing your time spent together on the new found purpose of the relationship—parents, co-workers, whatever that is. Try not to do things that would subvert or confuse the new relationship.

I'm not suggesting you act like an unemotional robot, either. You're human and it's likely you still love, or at least care about, this person. So there will be a transition involved. It will take time for you to think differently about who this person is to you. You both have to learn new roles and ways of talking and relating to each other. You are literally transitioning from one type of relationship to another. You may accept that in your mind, but your heart will usually be slower in adjusting. It wants what it wants and doesn't give up easily. So just be conscious of that and take your time.

In order to elaborate on this point a bit more, I reached out to a couple of people who know first hand what it takes to heal your broken heart while constantly having to be around the person who broke it—my parents! Yep. My parents. A little background: my parents grew up together in our church and fell in love at age 14. True story. They dated all through junior high and high school and into their twenties. Eventually, they got married, and a couple of years later they had me! I just love that story. People describe it as such a special thing to have watched—my parents' courtship. It was so predictable and storybook—until it wasn't.

They divorced when I was 3 ½. This was majorly tough for both of them and their respective families. And if dealing with being newly divorced, and all the hurt that comes with it, and trying to raise a child together post-divorce wasn't enough to figure out, they also had the added layer of being members of the same church. Oh and naturally both families were too. Dad was a regularly attending member. Mom was a member, pianist, and choir director. And then there was me, their little energetic daughter right there in the middle of all of it, growing up right there just as they had.

How in the world could they expect to heal, having to see each other so much? I wanted to know how they managed to do it. Because here it is nearly 30 years after their divorce, and we are all still members of the same church. In fact, my Dad remarried and my stepmom is a member too. So mom, dad, stepmom, and I are all there together Sunday after Sunday—and generally we get along. There's no real drama. We have our moments, but things typically go well. My mom and stepmom even talk to each other, share smiles and stories and basically get along well. But to get to where we are today, I know my parents had to take some action early on that allows for such peace now. So I asked them both to tell me what it was like in the first days after the divorce. What was their secret? How did they do it? How did they heal, while constantly looking in the face of the one who hurt them?

When I spoke to my mom and dad (separately), a few themes emerged in the course of our conversations.

MY TALK WITH MOM

Choose to be civil and communicate.

"The main thing for me was the fact that I knew that it was right to maintain some type of civil relationship because we had a child together. And no matter what I thought, or however he pissed me off, or what I didn't like, I knew I had to keep a line of communication open enough so if I needed to talk to him about our child, I could do that. And we did make a pact that we would always try to keep that line of communication open. We knew that was going to be necessary."

You and your ex may feel differently about the break up.

"And with regard to the idea of seeing him every week...I think I took that for granted because I was so used to seeing him. I never had this big issue with that. And I do believe that it was much harder for your dad than it was for me. And that's just what I believe. I think we were on two different pages when we approached the divorce. [Mom wanted the divorce. Dad didn't]. I think your dad went through more because he really did not want to lose his family. For me I wasn't seeing it as losing my family. At that point I had my daughter, and to not be married anymore wasn't that deep for me as it was for him... I really didn't grow up with a daddy in the house so that connection to that family piece just wasn't there for me. I think your daddy had more of a father figure in the house than I did. And it was a joy to be a part of that family thing. But I was able to disconnect myself from it without having a whole lot of issues. So seeing me at that time was probably more emotional for your dad. And that's why he always referred to our divorce as a rough divorce. He always told people that, but I disagreed with that."

Accept what you cannot control

"So seeing him on a regular basis was what I had gotten used to. Knowing that we grew up in the same church, it was my church [too] so I never felt out of place. Other people felt funny about it and they expressed it to me. The only thing that was weird for me was to watch your dad begin to date other women in the church. Because

I never dated anyone else in the church at all. So that meant I had to see him resurfacing and rebuilding his life in a way that reminded me of when it was me and him. The hardest thing for me was getting used to him dating other women in the church. I particularly, did not like that. But I was divorced so I didn't have the right to say anything."

Our child came first

"We both believed that our child came first. No matter what we felt individually we felt strongly about making sure that you had a peaceful life. And just because we decided to divorce we didn't want you to feel loved on one side [of your family] and not the other. That was never going to happen. And I don't think you've felt to this day you've ever felt unloved by either side. So we decided together spoken and unspoken, we assumed that role to make sure that you had as comfortable a life as you could with divorced parents."

MY TALK WITH MY DAD

Heartbreak is really tough.

"There's nothing like a heartache. And it's a heavy thing when you learn that you are not wanted. That hurts. That hurts. It's okay if you knew it up front and you went on with it knowing it was just a physical relationship, because people have those physical relationships. But when your heart's attached to it and your heart gets

stepped on, it hurts. So it takes some time to get through that process, but you learn how to deal with it day by day..."

Choose to get along.

"I think consciously she and I decided to get along. Just do the grown up thing and get along. This is what we needed to do because we had a child involved. [And our child] didn't have anything to do with any of this. So you just have to do that [resolve to get along] because otherwise that bitterness will kill you. You have to find a way to release the bitterness."

Release the bitterness.

"So I worked on myself and not becoming bitter because bitterness only destroys you. Even though there was some bitterness in me, I had to work on it and keep it under control because the best thing that came out of our relationship was our daughter. So therefore, I had to create a positive atmosphere for you. So whenever we interacted, it had to be positive. You just [have to] do it because kids do not ask to be a part of adult mess. They're just drafted into it. So that helped me.

"Also, I asked God to help me [release the bitterness] because I wasn't able to. If you don't address it, it will come out in various ways that you really may not be able to control it. It will eat you up. That bitterness? It will consume you. And I saw that happening to someone

once. And I thought, that could've been me. So the difference is Christ. I just had to give it to him."

"He said he'll take care of the hurt. He'll absorb that for you. We try to carry it, but we can't. We just can't. I literally cried tears behind my wife. I did—and that is not a manly thing to be saying. When I look back at it, it probably helped in the healing—the fact that I did cry. I know that it helped me....But if you do like Enoch, if you walk with God, God will walk with you and carry you through, God will help you get through all that stuff."

Choose to forgive and take responsibility for yourself.

"So what helped me, too, was, and it took awhile, but I learned to forgive her before she ever asked me to. Once I did that, I could feel the healing coming for me. And then I was convicted of my role in the destruction of the marriage. Because I never believed it was my fault...I blamed her for quite some time. But as I was drawn closer in my relationship to God, he revealed to me and showed it to me. I had an awakening. I realized that I played a part in the destruction of the marriage so I came and apologized to her and to you. In order for healing to take place, one has to own up to one's mess. You just have to own up to it! If it's yours, it's yours. If the other party doesn't forgive you, that's okay."

What I love about what my parents had to say was that

they both pointed to the choice they made to get along. This was the most powerful part of our conversations for me And it's so connected to what we've been discussing in this chapter about creating space. If complete physical space is not possible and you *have to be* in one another's space fairly regularly—because you have a child together, work together, have mutual friends, etc—*you can choose* to make your shared space more bearable, positive, and tolerable. If you must be around each other, choose to make it as positive an experience as can be. Don't fill that space and time together with negativity, distress, and more pain! Do the best you can to get along. At the core, it is a choice. And the choice to get along is simultaneously a choice to start healing. It will allow those wounds to get some air, to breathe. It will create the emotional climate necessary for healing to happen. Conversely, if you make a choice to fight, you are just reopening old wounds over and over, adding more pain on top of the pain already there. This will make healing impossible. If you have to spend any time together in any capacity, do yourself a favor, and choose to make it as positive as can be. Your heart will thank you later.

Again, none of this will be easy and it will take time. So be patient with yourself. Ask for the kind of support you need from loved ones. Please note: while I've given a lot of pointers here, always remember to assess your own needs and decide what really works for you. If you don't agree with something I've said, then you can try something different. It's your life after all. Make the decision that you think suits you best, and see how things go. The important part is for you to learn what actions you need to take for you to heal. I am more interested in your creating space and opportunity for healing in your life than anything else. So constantly assess your own needs as you journey and make adjustments accordingly.

QUIETNESS AS DEVOTION

I've mentioned numerous times now that the purpose of quietness is to "clear our headspace," or "give us clarity." We've talked about cutting down the noise in our world, creating some distance and space from people who've hurt us, but what are we supposed to do with all this space and quiet once we've achieved it? Quite simply: Be with God. This is what we've been building towards—restful, peaceful communion with the one who loves us unconditionally. The presence of God *is* your refuge from the chaos. That is the place of healing. Never leave God out of the equation. You need God's strength, power, and guidance to navigate these waters of heartbreak. So do invite and keep God as your coach in this process. Pray. Listen. Pray. Listen. Pray and listen some more. If you are looking for ways to spend time with God, check the resource section at the end of the book for ideas on how to do that.

I believe God, and God alone, is the healer of our every ill.[21] And the only way we will experience that

---

21 "Healer Of Our Every Ill" is a beautiful hymn written

healing is to make space for God in our hearts and lives. Think of those two healing passages we discussed earlier. In both instances, the man and the woman (in their own way) had to invite Jesus to heal them—the woman by pursuing, the man by allowing. They both had to demonstrate that Jesus was welcome. As we yearn for wholeness and healing, we must invite God into those broken corridors of our hearts to do the miraculous, mysterious work of healing in our lives.

This is why the quiet and space are so critical! We have to move other stuff out (noise, certain people, unhealthy activity, etc.) so that we can make room for God. How can we hear God if our mind is so crowded with everyone else's advice? How can we experience God's presence if we're constantly in the presence of the one who hurt us. That stuff has to go, for a while, so God has room to enter in and begin God's creative, powerful healing work in us. Make room for God to dwell in the cold, dark, lonely, painful corners of your heart. And here is the coolest part about all of this: God actually *wants* to be there!

"God is our refuge and strength, a very present help in the time of trouble."
Psalm 46:1

---

by Marty Haugen which beautifully conveys God as a compassionate Healer who deeply understands and empathizes with human pain. GIA, Inc Publications, 1987.

Pause and let that sink in for a minute. Who else do you know that wants to be present in your pain with you? Listen, I am a minister and it is terribly uncomfortable, clergy person that I am, to be present with someone when they're hurting. When someone I know loses a loved one, I never know what to say, what to do. I can pray, show up, bring food, and other supplies, but I always feel so incompetent, like it's not enough. I never can get past the look of hurt in their eyes; it pains my heart sometimes to the point of paralysis. Every act of kindness I seek to offer is uncomfortable for me: making a call, asking how they're doing, it's just a painful thing for me because I just hate seeing my loved ones in pain. It's really tough and terribly uncomfortable to be present with someone who is hurting, and sometimes I'd prefer to avoid them altogether. In all honesty, sometimes I have. I know others feel this way too; it's human.

But God purposefully steps into our painful realities, powerfully and boldly, unintimidated by our trauma, unafraid of our pain, and ready to help. Can you imagine it? God actually wants to be with us in our darkest, most depressed, most hopeless moments. Notice it's not just that God is there, but God actually *wants to* be there! That blows my mind every time I think of it. Nobody actually *wants* to enter those dark, ugly places with us. We do it, but I'm not sure we want to. If we could just remove a person's pain altogether, then I think we'd much prefer that. And even when our closest loved ones, our ride-or-die truest-bluest friends are actually courageous enough to walk through those darkest moments of pain with us, it can be overwhelming for them, much more than they themselves can handle.

God, however, has no problem stepping right in at the point of our need, in the midst of the worst kind of sorrow. Now I don't mean to paint God as some sadistic deity that actually enjoys our painful moments, but rather as a deeply compassionate savior, lover, and healer who cares enough to show up when we're at our worst. That's a reason to shout! When you're in that space that hurts the most, the hurt so deep it keeps you up at night, that's where God *wants* to be—right there with you!

"It is of the LORD'S mercies that we are not consumed, because his compassions fail not. They are new every morning: great is thy faithfulness."
Lamentations 3:22-23 (King James Version)

So take solace in this: When you create that space and cut down the chatter in your world, you are actually making room for God. As you remove all the clutter from your heart, mind, and spirit, God moves in and plans to hold you, console you, and love you! In this, God is your "refuge," giving you a hiding place away from the people and situation that hurt you. God's presence becomes a reprieve, a resting place for your heart.

In one of my favorite devotional books, Jesus Calling, Sarah Young so beautifully describes how God's presence refreshes and renews us...

"Let the dew of My Presence refresh your mind and heart. So many, many things vie for your attention in this complex world of instant communication. The world has changed enormously since I first gave the command to be still and know that I am God. However, this timeless trust is essential for the well-being of your soul. As dew refreshes grass and flowers during the stillness of the night, so My Presence revitalizes you as you sit quietly with Me. *A refreshed, revitalized mind is able to sort out what is important and what is not. In its natural condition, your mind easily* gets *stuck on trivial matters. Like the spinning wheels of a car trapped in mud, the cogs of your brain spin impotently when you focus on a trivial thing. As soon as you start communicating with Me about the matter, your thoughts gain traction and you can move on to more important things. Communicate with Me continually, and I will put My thoughts into your mind."* [22]

This beautiful picture Sarah paints here describes what happens for us once God moves into our space. First, she notes that God's presence refreshes us. This is absolute truth. I love that word "refresh," it's all about being energized and renewed. It's like that cool glass of water after you've been sweating in the hot sun all day. That cool sensation trickles down your throat, gently cooling your insides, and restoring strength to your entire body. It's that unplanned Sunday afternoon nap.

---

22 Young, Sarah. *Jesus Calling: Enjoying Peace in His Presence.* Nashville: Thomas Nelson, 2004, 258.

It's that delicious lunch during a draining work day that reenergizes you for the hours remaining. It's that perfect hug from a loved one who squeezes you, reminding you of your worth and that you're loved. Refreshment is so vital to our lives, and God steps into the midst of our pain to provide it.

And my, don't we need refreshment, in the midst of this horrible pain? Heartbreak tends to shake us at the very core of our being, make us question everything. Am I worthy of love? How did I get here? What did I do wrong? Why is this happening? Will I ever find the love I want? These are real questions worth examining in order for us to learn and grow, but as long as we're in a hurt, painful place, it is difficult to think clearly. It's like those spinning wheels of a car stuck in mud that Sarah Young describes in the devotion above. There are no answers. Just pain. Disappointment. Shock. Disbelief. Sadness. We are broken, confused, stuck, and in need of something to revitalize us from the inside-out, to transform us. We need God's presence to refresh us, to blow a cool breeze of love to calm our spirits, to begin to bind up our broken hearts.

And all of this can be scary. I know. What does it mean to really open up and allow God in, really? It can seem like an invasion. Our vulnerability and our pain can make us reluctant to let anyone in when we're hurting, even God. But remember that God is the healer of our every ill, the only one who can truly make us whole. Don't fear because God is a loving, faithful, and trustworthy God. God's desire is not to harm you but to help you. So trust God's presence is a *safe* space. This loving presence won't bring heartbreak, won't force you to move faster than you're ready, won't even ridicule you for poor choices. Even if you suspect that you are at fault for what happened, God won't tear you down for that, not in this space. Here God only wants to mend you, heal you, and bind up your brokenness. There is no need to fear, but if you do, God's grace will meet you there anyway. Let me now share a story of a really horrifying and deeply painful time in my life. I had broken my own heart, but God stepped into the pain with me and I experienced God's radical mercy. And I'll never forget it.

I remember it like it was yesterday. I was standing on the corner waiting for the bus headed to work. My heart started beating fast when I looked down at my phone and saw I had a missed call from my doctor's office. I hadn't been feeling really well for a few days and I was waiting on some test results. Nothing could have prepared me for the news I was about to receive. Tears rolled down my face as I listened to the message the nurse left on my voicemail, "Ms. Williams you tested positive for an STD. Please call us as we need to get you in right away for treatment." I could not BELIEVE I'd done this to myself. My mind wouldn't rest. "How could I? Why did I? What's gonna' happen?" Thankfully, in my case it was curable, but it was still an STD! "How could I have let this happen?!?!?!?" But I had. Yep, church girl, Jesus lover, singing and praising Arionne had an STD. I felt low, lower than I'd ever felt in my life. It was as real as real can be.

What was most amazing about that experience was that I never felt anything from God but pure love. The mercy of God was so incredible. I kept waiting for God's judgment to crush me, or to be overcome by divine anger, or faint from the sheer terror of God's wrath—at least, suffer a lash or two. But that moment never happened. I knew what poor choices I'd made and really didn't need to be reminded of them. What I needed was to know that I was still loved by God, despite my shortcomings. I needed to be affirmed, loved, and made whole. And God did just that. I clearly heard God say to me, "You are the same person with the same mission. I forgive you. And I love you." And God was right, I hadn't changed. I was who God said I was and nothing or no person, not even I, could change that.

It was amazing, the idea that God entered one of my darkest moments, not to chide, punish, or condemn, but simply to love. God reassured me, mended my heart, rebuilt my confidence, helped me get up and move on. I wasn't left to drown in my pain because, at my invitation, God entered my dark place and transformed my reality.

"For the Lord your God is living among you. He is a mighty savior. He will take delight in you with gladness.
With his love, he will calm all your fears.
He will rejoice over you with songs."
Zephaniah 3:17 (New Living Translation)

To be sure, some others may try to use your mistakes as a way to tell you you're not all you pretend to be. One person very close to me did just that. And it HURT! Know that these attacks are designed to keep you hurting, feeling low, and perpetually in pain. So don't give these words any credence. None. Frankly, it is outright dangerous to allow such words to have power and influence on you in the midst of your heartbreaking situation. You'll never heal taking in their poison.

In contrast, God's presence is love and compassion made real—that means it's safe. There is no need to fear. The "god" people love to describe who judges, punishes, and lashes out never showed up in my situation. The experience was an eye-opener for me, a reminder of who I really was, and a clear indication that I needed to change my risky behavior; but what I felt more than anything was God's love and mercy. As a result, rather than running from God in the midst of my pain, I ran *to* God who, with open arms, welcomed me, my pain, my humiliation, my brokenness, my STD, and all. And those arms became my place of healing, my solace, and my restoration.

Note how my choice to accept what happened led to healing on all levels, physical, spiritual, and emotional. Once I acknowledged my diagnosis, I got the medical care I needed. My STD was cured and I was completely healthy a few weeks later..Moreover, my acceptance of what had happened allowed me to be honest with God, who saw my pain, and healed me of my guilt and shame, and restored me emotionally and spiritually.

And how exactly does it happen? How does God heal us? What tools and processes are put into effect? I have to admit that I have no idea. God's incredible work of healing in our lives is a miraculous thing which we cannot explain. It's a sheer mystery how God breaks into our dismal reality, penetrating to the core of the war-torn battleground of our hearts, rebuilding and restoring everything that was damaged or destroyed. We cannot begin to imagine how it happens, what it really takes, and how much love God really pours on us, but that is perfectly okay. We don't need to fully comprehend it and we won't. For God's thoughts are not our thoughts and our ways are not God's ways. "For just as the heavens are higher than the earth, so my ways higher than your ways and my thoughts are higher than your thoughts," says the Lord through the prophet Isaiah (55:8). And this is actually a relief. We don't have to be able to explain or understand how God heals us, and we aren't responsible for our own healing. Our role is simply to trust God *for the* healing. And this is God's sacred work, not ours. We just need to be faithful to the parts we can do—accept, be transparent, be silent.

Moreover, this divine work of healing is real and sure. For what God begins in you, God is certain to complete in you. It may take time, but stay with it. God, who has begun a good work in you will complete it until the day of Jesus Christ (Philippians 1:6). This is God's promise to you. If you allow God in to begin a work of healing in you, God will finish the job. God's work is guaranteed. God is not some shady contractor who comes in, takes your money, does shoddy unreliable work, and has to come back and fix it year after year. When God starts the work of healing, know that God will complete it.

Your only job is to open up and let God in to work in you daily. It's like the good contractor that comes to your home every morning to supervise the repair work. Keep letting her in so she can ensure the job gets done right. Let God dwell in your heart, rule in your mind to do the powerful work of healing, always remembering that it is God's work. That's key. Never think you are going to fix your own heart. So let the process begin. Open your heart. Let God in. Rest in God's presence. And be healed.

QUIETNESS OVER TIME

Finally, be patient with yourself in this process. People like to say that "time heals all wounds," but let me offer this correction: Healing takes time. I walked around for weeks with a heaviness that weighed my heart down so low, I swore it dragged the floor when I walked. It hurt for a long while. But eventually it got better, but that wasn't just because the time passed.

"because you know that the testing of your faith produces endurance. And let endurance have its full effect

so that you may be mature and complete, lacking in nothing."
James 2:3-4

The truth is people often carry hurts for years over long periods of time, and are never healed. They are just as hurt after 3 years as they were on day one. They develop coping strategies, cover-ups, poker faces, masks, and all other kinds of devices to hide their pain. But hiding doesn't equal healing. So time doesn't heal anything. Only God does. But if you've opened yourself to God's healing, know that it's not an instantaneous experience. No magic. No tricks here. It's really just the daily process of your allowing God into your broken space. Let that process continually happen over time and you will get there. Allow that quietness and let the fresh air of God's presence into your broken place every day until you're healed.

CHOOSE YOUR FUTURE

The final question then really is: Do you want this? Do you really want to be healed? Remember Jesus asked the man at the pool, "Sir, do you want to be healed?" God dwells where God is invited. The Lord wants to heal you and will. The question is will you invite God to do it? And at this point in our discussion, I think it's helpful if you sit and reflect upon that question: Do you really want this? I know. I know. That question sounds just as ridiculous now as it did when Jesus posed it to the gentleman sick for 38 years? But don't blow that question off too fast.

You must decide that you really want to change for the better. You have to determine that you want a different experience. This will mean letting go of some things that have become comforting and familiar to you. This means you will have to be open to a new way of living and being, leaving behind some old beliefs, attitudes, and feelings. Believe me, there's a better, healed, and happy you that you can step into, but you have to want it. That's it. That's all. Just want it. And when you can say yes to really wanting it, then you really are in position and ready for a miraculous experience of healing in your life.

And listen, everyone is different. You do not have to be like home girl who ran like crazy when she saw Jesus pass through town! I have to admit, for a long time, I always thought a little higher of her than I did the man at the pool. I loved her initiative and the way that she never gave up, even after twelve years. She let nothing get between her and her healing, not the social conventions (which limited male and female contact), religious leaders and their rules, the disciples, the crowds, nobody! And if this is you and you can relate to her then I say to you, "Go GET WHAT'S YOURS!!!" Run after your healing! Go 'head!

But if this isn't your story, and you find yourself lying by the pool, only imagining a happier, healed you, having frustrated yourself trying to figure out how you can get into your pool, know that God hasn't neglected you. Perhaps you've been trying to heal but the methods you've employed just haven't worked. Maybe all the let downs through the years and all the feelings of failure from your attempts to move past the hurt have drained all your energy. Maybe it's you lying in the porches of Sheep Gate, having secretly resigned that you just may have to live with this pain the rest of your life.

Is this you? Be honest. If so, I have good news for you: You don't have to get up and run to meet Jesus in the crowd. You don't even have to find a way to get yourself into the pool. God meets you at *your* Sheep Gate, ready, willing, and able to heal your broken heart. All you have to do is say yes. You may not have the energy to put on your track shoes and run to get your healing, but you don't have to. Jesus will show up and meet you right where you are—this is God's grace made real in your life! You just need enough energy to say yes to God in whatever way you know how. Just be willing. God will begin a work of healing in you.

One More Caveat...
DEVELOP A SUPPORT SYSTEM

I wanted to talk briefly about this idea of a support system, having some people assembled that you can call in place, in life in general. We all know that there is some pain involved in living. A lot of times we think that we can handle all this stuff ourselves, or if we just pray, everything will be okay. Although I just shared two long chapters on prayer, I want to advocate for therapy, counseling, psychiatry, and spiritual direction as great options to be paired with the work of our prayer lives.

Truly God does gift mental wellness professionals in such a way that they are able to help people walk through difficult moments and process some of life's traumas in healthy, productive ways. Unfortunately there are still stigmas in our society around seeking professional counseling, and these methods aren't always celebrated in the church. I believe the mental wellness profession is an example of God's provision. In fact, counseling and its counterparts are a way of partaking of the bounty that is available to you, the resources that God has provided for us. Use it. Seek it out. I did. It helps. Please see the resource section at the end of the book to begin exploring what spiritual, mental, and emotional health support is right for you.

From Prison to Paradise[23]

As the days moved on, slowly, but surely, so did I. Over time, God absolutely healed me. As I continually, daily practiced acceptance, transparency (lament), and quiet, I was healed. I wish I could pinpoint each turn to describe more articulately the process of healing, but I cannot. All I know is I kept living, kept breathing, kept hoping for better and eventually, I experienced healing, I also handed over my broken pieces to God, eventually I felt restored and renewed at the same time. I know God did the healing when I yielded.

The following chapter further outlines the lessons I learned during my journey from heartbreak prison to paradise.

23 I am indebted to Queenie Johnson of the She Rises School of Success for Women for this term.

PART III LESSONS AND REFLECTIONS IN THE AFTERMATH

CHAPTER SEVEN WHEN CLARITY COMES

Lesson #1 There Are No Rules In Love

When Jamaal and I first met and started to get to know each other, I thought of him as a possible life partner. While at some very faint, subconscious level I had doubts, Jamaal really was everything I wanted and everything I had been looking for. He was intelligent, handsome, a gentleman, a Christian, well-read, cultured, kind-hearted, fun, and adventurous— we had a great time together. The fit just felt so right. He was really a great guy. He courted me. He was very confident in his approach to me. He called me often and showed serious interest in me. He was consistent in making plans to spend time with me. And he made it clear that he was very interested in me and definitely wanted to be with me.

He was very different from other guys that I had dated before. In prior experiences, I'd always had an inkling that it might not work out. There was always some tension or issue that we just could not seem to resolve, preventing those relationships from getting off the ground. I remember dating one guy and we fought all the time. He was always suspicious of me. This made it hard for me do anything right in his eyes. So no matter how much I may have wanted it to work, I had this unsettled feeling deep inside that said: "this ain't gon' work."

But with Jamaal, it was different because we really didn't have any conflict. Everything was going along just fine. He approached me with confidence. He was sure of himself and he was straight up with me about what he wanted. He wasn't playing a bunch of games. In other words he was a *very grown man* about what he was doing. He didn't let me wonder about other women. I wasn't worried about whether he was serious or playing or if he was just trying to "get some." He made it very clear from the very beginning that he wanted a relationship.

So when all of a sudden it was over, I was like, "WHAT? Is he freaking kidding me? Like, really?" It just came out of the clear blue sky. That was why he was such a challenge and that heartbreak was so harsh because it literally came out of nowhere. And we had just talked about the relationship a few weeks prior. We'd discussed whether or not we were both happy and our expectations. During that conversation, he did indicate that he didn't feel madly in love yet. And I said to him, "Well, Jamaal, it's still early yet, we shouldn't necessarily be madly in love yet. I'm not even sure that's even normal this early. I think we'll grow to that." And that was that. We didn't talk anymore about it. In retrospect, I should have listened to him a bit more and taken his concerns more seriously.

That's another thing that we really need to examine

as we think about expectations for our relationships. Is it really true that people just literally fall in love or do they grow? Does it happen the same way with everybody all the time? Does it feel exactly the same for everybody? What does love and being in love look like for different people?

In our case, I think Jamaal expected our relationship to develop much quicker than it did; perhaps he thought those "magical" feelings should be in place early. He was very clear about what his intentions were and what he wanted, so he dove in very deep, very hard, very quickly. He was ready, pretty early on, to make things official. He told me, "I'm ready to be with you. I want to date you exclusively." So I had to slow him down, "Whoa, I'm not ready to be in a relationship yet." I was just so grateful to have met such a great guy. I was enjoying the courting and mutual affection and participation that I'd not experienced in a long time. And it really was the first time I'd met someone who wanted to give back and share love together. With so many other guys, there was no reciprocity and I was used to coming up short. So I was enjoying the ride for awhile. I was in la-la land so high off of how things were going that I didn't notice that the two of us were in different places. His outlook was different from mine. He was ready to move full speed ahead and I just wasn't there yet.

To be honest, we got along great and had a lot of things in common. It was so perfect. The fit was so nice; it was like "where have you been?" And he even said that to me once, "I've been looking for you high and low, far and wide. Where have you been? I've been looking for you." And I was like, "YES!!!, I've been looking for you too!"

So when we finally came together, it felt like everything that I wanted. This was what I prayed for and I finally had it! Though if I am completely honest, deep, deep down, the Lord was telling me *"this ain't necessarily it."* At the time, I did not recognize this as God's voice. I only realized it in hindsight. During the relationship itself, I just knew that I was not totally settled with the idea of our relationship being a forever-kind-of-thing just yet. At the time though, I was content with continuing to enjoy our time together and I just didn't give much more than a passing thought to that feeling I had. For me, this was still a very enjoyable experience. We were going along and things were just fine, nearly perfect in my book. There should not have been this huge let down, but it just came out of nowhere. He's like, "I have no more feelings for you." And that's why the hurt in that case was worse than it had ever been.

However, when I considered that whole relationship a little closer, I realized that I was not as crazy about him as I had been about other guys I'd dated. I was crazier about the circumstances and what happened and how he pursued me than I was about him, even though I did like him. I really did like him, but I can think of at least one other person that I liked more—a lot more—in terms of the person, my attraction to him, and how he made me feel whenever I was around him. After I began to experience healing and I reflected back on the experience, I realized that it was the *circumstances* with Jamaal that made me excited, interested, and happy. He took the right steps and made the right moves, but he ultimately wasn't the right person. And I need the right person to make the right moves at the right time. And sometimes you might have the right person but they can't make the right moves because it's not the right time. Or they just won't make the right move. They have all the qualities, what you want, what you need, what's interesting, what works for you, what turns you on and gets you excited, but they won't take the right steps. Jamaal was willing to take the steps but then later decided, "I don't really want this." I'm not sure that's any better, because you still end up with heartbreak!

That's why sometimes I am very wary of people who speak very generally, in a cliché kind of way about relationships as if there are all these hard fast rules. "If he calls you then he really wants you. And if he doesn't call you then he's really not that into you." This love business is just too dynamic and unpredictable for these oversimplifications of human behavior.

But that doesn't stop people from sharing some of this unhelpful, stereo-typical "wisdom" all over the place. Now with social media, everybody is a philosopher. Everyone is an expert. Everyone is a scholar, psychiatrist or psychologists. Everybody's a minister. Social media provides people with this automatic 24-hour audience.

So they can just jump on Twitter, Facebook, Tumbler, Instagram, or whatever and suddenly become an authority on relationships. And people read this and take this stuff as true, living their lives by it! And I think you should always have your critical eyes open. I just don't go for some of the stuff I read about relationships online. "If you do x,y,z, this that or the other will happen," as if there's just this formula that will help you figure it all out. 1+2=3. Not in love, baby! In love, relationships, and dating, when you're dealing with people and their desires, wants, needs, insecurities, issues, drama, baggage, honey, 2+2 might mean 14. It might mean -7. Everything just does not add up mathematically. It's not a formula.

Get this: Jamaal approached me correctly. He did all the right things. He courted me; he got to know me. And he wasn't just running game. I believe he had a genuine interest in developing a long-lasting relationship with me, but perhaps that interest is not enough. Our breakup was so hurtful at the time because this was not supposed to happen with *him*. He was the guy that made all the right moves. He was the guy that did all the right things, but it still did not work out.

So, you cannot assume that just because someone is consistent, and genuine, and taking all the necessary steps, that you will have your happily ever after. No! That's not life. You have no idea what's going to happen because it's so dynamic and volatile. Nothing is really that stable. People change their minds, their feelings shift, they find something they are more interested in and things change. This does not mean that real love is not possible or long lasting. It means that sometimes things just don't work out the way you think they should. I learned with Jamaal that even when it looks like the perfect match, and everything fits, and you get along and it feels good, it still may not turn out to be what you want. And you won't have any control over that. The real question is: how will you adjust? Your focus is now on how you can heal and move forward.

Lesson #2 "Life Doesn't Get Easier...You Get Stronger"

My good friend Jon gave me this really good advice when I was in the thick of working through the hurt after the breakup with Jamaal. He shared about the time he and his wife Michelle were going through this intense fitness boot camp. They had to be at the gym at 5am every morning, Monday through Friday, for three weeks; he said it was the hardest, most intense workout out of their lives! It was extremely difficult. The first couple of days, Jon was like, "I can't do this. This is crazy. Why do I keep showing up? This is just way too hard!" Somehow, though, they stuck with it. As time went on, Jon said that he kept expecting bootcamp to get easier, but what he was finding was that it wasn't any easier at all. In fact, the workouts were just as intense and difficult on day 10 as they were on day 2, but the difference was that they were stronger. In class he kept saying, "This is still some BS! This is still a really hard workout! It's not getting any easier." And the instructor had said to them, "It doesn't get easier; you just get stronger." Those words rang completely true for me during that time in my life.

The pain was more intense than it had ever been in comparison to other heartbreaks that I'd experienced for a couple of reasons. First of all, I had no idea it was coming—literally NO IDEA! So the pain was more intense, in part, because I didn't expect it. Consequently, I didn't have a chance to brace myself for the hit I was about to take. Furthermore, *I had already been through a ton* of let downs and disappointments before with other guys. I knew love unrequited all too well. It had been my painful reality for nearly all of my twenties. So *surely*, I was going to win this time! I mean, wasn't it my turn? I was certain that this was my time for love! My expectations were super high.

So when suddenly it was over, the pain was epic, worse than it had ever been. It was like I was reliving all those other heartbreaks again. This hurt was deep and bellowing. And it was unrelenting. It was like somebody was playing a cruel joke on me, staying around to taunt me: "See, it didn't work this time either! You're right back where you don't want to be: Heartbroken! Ha-ha-ha-ha-ha!" Jamaal couldn't have known that his departure would cause this depth of sorrow, but it really shook me to the core, causing a crisis of faith. This wasn't just emotional; it was spiritual. The pain was so deep, the groans so low, I know only the Holy Spirit could understand them.

So the pain was really intense, but the interesting part about it was that it didn't last very long. I recovered quicker. I distinctly remember driving home from work one day and suddenly I thought, "Wow. Today I actually feel like Arionne." And I hadn't felt that in almost a month. It took some time, but I still healed from that hurt faster, even though it was the worst hurt I ever felt from a breakup. Now how amazing is that? It was the worst heartbreak, but my fastest recovery. How is that even possible?

The truth was my heart had already been through quite a workout. It was a harder hit, this time but I could take it because I was stronger. My past experiences of disappointment had made me tougher and better able to withstand the blow. And it didn't kill me. I got through it Also I knew what it would take to get through this. So I immediately started to do what I needed to do to care for myself. So my past hurtful experiences served me well by equipping me with the tools of survival. So it really is true that life does not get any easier. The hits keep coming, but you really do get stronger.

That's the only encouraging thing about heartbreaks; if you pay attention to the lessons, and allow yourself to heal, you do get tougher. God knows a lot of us are going to go through multiple ones in our lifetimes. It's not that we're looking forward to it, but love and relationships are such volatile business. You just never have any idea what the hell is going to happen at any given moment. Even when people make a commitment to get married and stay married 50 years. Even in that, there's a lot of volatility. My Godfather would say that, "Life starts coming at you fast." You just have no idea; stuff comes out of nowhere. It's just like a roller coaster: you're going along just fine and then all of a sudden, there's a drop and you did not see it coming. Know, though, that you definitely have what it takes get through it because your past experiences made you stronger and prepared you for what you have to deal with this time.

Lesson #3 Have The Critical Conversations

I also learned that before beginning a new relationship, it's important to sit down and talk to your partner about what exactly you both are expecting. When you are trying to figure out whether or not this relationship is going to be a success, what will help you determine what success looks like? What are your barometers? When you evaluate "Is it worthy of my time to continue this," what are the criteria, what are you looking for? What are you looking to feel and experience in this relationship? How do you know when it is love? What makes you know that this is something that you want? Share those things together.

You could both be looking for two different things and maybe that's okay, but I think it's important that you are both of aware of what you looking for. This is not so the other person can try to change who they are and meet your expectations in an unnatural way. Rather it is so you two can come together and decide what you want and what you're trying to accomplish and experience together. That was part of the problem with Jamaal. I think he had an unrealistic expectation. I had a different kind of expectation. I was not worried about feeling madly in love with Jamaal right off the bat, but he was. He was looking for some major things to happen a lot sooner than I was. For me it was all about growing into it and just enjoying the experience. What does a successful, happy, healthy relationship look like for the two of you? What you create together might not be the same as what you would create with someone else. The expectations are going to be different; the desires, what you want, might be different in some ways. You develop those things as a couple. So it's important to talk through that.

Ultimately, I have realized that Jamaal and I started the relationship way too soon. Frankly, we had only dated for about a month and a half when we made our relationship official. He later told me after the breakup that he'd felt a sense of urgency because he didn't want me to be with somebody else, not because he was really crazy about me. I was actually shocked to hear this. All that time when he kept pressing me to get into a relationship with him, he was doing so because he just didn't want anyone else to have me. I think that's a natural feeling, but it shouldn't be the whole story. How about being with someone because you like who they are, you enjoy their company, you can't imagine not having them in your life? But to do it just because you don't want anyone else to have them? Ummm. No. That's not gonna' cut it. Be with me because you want me and for no other reason. So really I don't think our relationship was based on the right things. It really should be based on "I want you and you want me." So that was another challenge for us that may have been come up earlier if we'd had some critical conversations.

Perhaps we were doomed to fail from the beginning. It could've been that if we had just kept dating and had more conversation about our expectations before we entered the relationship, we may have figured out that this really wasn't going anywhere. Yes, it was super exciting because of how it developed, we had a lot in common, and everything seemed to just fit so nicely, but perhaps if we had taken more time we would've figured out before we were in a relationship that this was not going to work.

See my Relationship Readiness Interview and Reflection Guide in the resource section for guidance on how to learn from past relationship experiences, and prepare for the next adventure in love!

Lesson #4 Love Takes Time To Heal

Confession. For several months after the break up: I really missed Jamaal. We'd had so much fun, I enjoyed his company, being around him, and having someone to talk to everyday at the end of the day. I enjoyed having someone to go hang out with, grab dinner with or just be with, I enjoyed his companionship. After I got over the initial shock of the break up and I got to the place where I felt like myself again, I was feeling better and my healing had really started to take place; but I was still thinking: *Damn, I miss him.*

This is natural. Don't fight it. It's going to take a while to get used to the change.

I wish I could give you a secret that would ease this pain of missing your beloved, but there is no such thing. As I continued to practice acceptance by acknowledging the end of the relationship (not trying to rewrite history), created space by not being in touch or hanging out with him, and met God in my quiet place, I slowly got used to him being gone. I probably didn't listen to love songs for a while. I didn't go places that reminded me of us. And I didn't spend a ton of time talking about him and what happened. Most importantly, whatever feelings of "missing him" that came up inside me, I honored them by acknowledging them. One thing my mom has always told me, "Don't ever be ashamed of your feelings." So I wasn't. I missed him and that was okay to feel. So if those feelings surfaced with tears, in anger, or however, I let them come up and flow out of me. I did not resist. Finally, I was patient. I gave my heart time to accept the change. It took awhile, but I got there.

CHAPTER EIGHT TAKE AWAY THOUGHTS... FINDING MY RESOLVE

Open Your Heart

*"You've abandoned me. Love don't live here anymore.
Just a vacancy.
Love don't live here anymore."*
—Rolls Royce on "Love Don't Live Here Anymore" from "Rolls Royce III: Strikes Again"

When you start to think you might be ready to move on, it's normal to try to talk yourself out of it. Sometimes it can be easier to decide just not to like people, to decide to close your heart off just so you won't get hurt again. You don't want to feel the pain again. You don't want to deal with the rejection. And even though its fun to like somebody, it's not fun when they don't respond the way you want them to, when they don't seem to be as into you as you are into them. It can be a little much. So sometimes you might say, "I'm not doing this." And that's an honest way to feel, but it probably isn't the healthiest outlook to have. The big thing is to be aware of it.

Don't choose not to love because of what you've already been through in your past. You don't want to allow old hurts to keep you from the bright and beautiful future that you daydream about—because it does exist. It won't be without flaws. Whoever you choose to love won't be a perfect individual, and neither will you. Your circumstances may not necessarily be ideal; it may not all work out exactly the way you planned but it can still be something beautiful and be exactly what you need. Hold out for that. Don't give up on what you want the most, on what you've fought the hardest to have because of a few setbacks.

Rather, give yourself permission and allow yourself the space to heal so that you *can* get to your happy. I guarantee you won't get there if you haven't healed. If you're carrying a bunch of baggage from your past, then nobody will want to go anywhere with you! (Shout out to Erykah Badu and her "Bag Lady!) You've got to work through your stuff. Be healed, honey! Until then you're not even in a position to recognize or see the love you really want anyway. You can't even respond to it properly. You can't appreciate or experience the good you are destined to experience if you are overwhelmed, drowning in pain. So there is work to be done to get through our pain. The blessing is that we don't do it alone. God is with us. There was no way I could have made it through my many heartbreaks and pains without God's healing. God is strengthening us and blessing us through the power of divine healing. I absolutely believe in that. Do you?

FORGIVE YOURSELF

In this book, I have not sought to blame people for their own pain, or to suggest that you must have done something to deserve this, but I do think there is something valuable in owning our own stuff. We do share some responsibility in what we go through. Perhaps you stayed in a relationship much longer than you should have, prolonging the break up, in a sense, choosing to be unhappy. Sometimes we choose things that we know aren't good for us from the start. Taking some ownership in what happened is critical to the healing itself. If you can't be honest about what happened, I'm not sure how you can heal. So really if your action is the reason, or even part of the reason, why you got hurt, you need to be honest about that and own it.

At the same time, while you do take responsibility for you action, you have to also be forgiving of yourself and not be angry for having made the decision you made. You made the choice for a whole number of reasons. And now you've learned and grown, so you've gained something. You didn't totally lose. There may have been a loss but it's not a total loss. In fact, it's never a total loss. You can always get better. You can always improve. You can always grow from the experience. That's the piece that excites me is that it's possible to grow from this. See the reflection guide in the resource section in the back of the book for more guidance on being self-reflective.

Though it's very easy to beat yourself up and feel

really horrible about what you did, I challenge you to resist that tendency. It's so completely unproductive and unhealthy. Shame and guilt get you nowhere and keep you stuck so don't hang on to them for too long. Sometimes, you made the decision because you didn't know. On the other hand, in some instances you definitely knew, "This is stupid and I should not do this," but you chose to move forward anyway. It was what you wanted to do. There's a whole number of reasons why you chose the path you did, but it's important to be self-forgiving. You made the choice. Accept it. Forgive yourself for it. Decide that it's okay to have made a poor decision, no matter how bad you think it was. Instead, focus on finding the positive in this. Ask yourself: What did I learn from this? How can I benefit from this? What can I gain from this experience? What wisdom did I attain? And how does this make me stronger and smarter and better for the next time around?

So you screwed it up. So what?!?!?! Sometimes you win and sometimes you learn! *They say*—I know, I know, the infamous "they"—that most often it's the things you *didn't* do in life that you live to regret, not the things you *did* do. So relax. Forgive yourself. Learn. Heal. Move on. Your life is waiting for you.

TOWARDS THE LOVE WE WANT...

Relationships Are ~~Volatile~~ An Adventure

I've talked a lot about the volatility of love and relationships and how at any moment anything could pop off. All hell could break loose without a moment's notice, but that's the adventure of living life with someone. That's the chance you take when you decide to love. You are opening yourself up to a whole heap of possibilities—some good, some not so good. In life you are going to have plenty of drama and your own stuff to deal with, but it's twice the fun when you're in a relationship because you not only have your stuff but your mates' stuff too—and that can be more than a notion. At the same time it's a blessing because now you're sharing those experiences together and that journey together can really be a beautiful thing.

And even though all kinds of things can go crazy and horribly wrong, things can go crazy and wonderfully well. That's the adventure of it. As much as there are low times and down times, there surely are good times and high times— when life really is good, the universe is properly aligned, and things are right (finally!) and the relationship and the love that you have is everything you could have ever imagined. Does the good outweigh the bad? That's a question you'll have to ask and answer for your own relationship. But never stop living! Live your life! Go ahead. LIVE! Inspired by the lyrics of singer-songwriter, Leann Womack, my mama would say to you,

Dance, baby! Dance!
I Hope You Dance
I hope you never lose your sense of wonder,

You get your fill to eat but always keep that hunger,
May you never take one single breath for granted,
God forbid love ever leave you empty handed,
I hope you still feel small when you stand beside the ocean,
Whenever one door closes I hope one more opens,
Promise me that you'll give faith a fighting chance,
And when you get the choice to sit it out or dance,
I hope you dance....I hope you dance.
I hope you never fear those mountains in the distance,
Never settle for the path of least resistance
Living might mean taking chances but they're worth taking
Loving might be a mistake but it's worth making
Don't let some hell bent heart leave you bitter,
When you come close to selling out reconsider,
Give the heavens above more than just a passing glance,
And when you get the choice to sit it out or dance.
I hope you dance....I hope you dance.
Time is a wheel in constant motion always rolling us along,
Tell me who wants to look back on their years and wonder where those years have gone.

WHAT I NEED IN MY MAN

"In my dating adventures I've learned that my personality requires a man who is not ego-obsessed, is secure, and does not feel threatened by a woman in the spotlight, yet still strong enough to hold his own such that I will respect him. I need someone with quiet strength that I can rely on and be vulnerable with in my moments of weakness, but who roots me on and is turned on when he sees me in my strongest, most powerful moments." –A text I once sent to my sister, Dominique.

Even though I've learned these are some of the things I need, it can be difficult to stay true to that when I really like somebody. 'Cause when you like somebody, you don't care. All reason and common sense goes out the window! But maybe there's grace even in that. Because perhaps we don't always know what we really need anyway. What I've learned is that dating is really all about learning. You cannot enter every situation thinking "he's the one." Nine times out of ten, he is not. What he could be though is an opportunity for you to explore yourself, how you love, and what you want.

Take me, for example. Each of the men that I've dated and spent time getting to know had some quality that I really want in a life partner. It's like I've met my husband over and over again, but just pieces of him in each man I've known. None of them really had all the qualities—at least, not that I recognized. They were all missing a piece or two. Jamaal was the first time I'd seen most of the qualities in one man. So he really looked like the one, *felt* like the one. He had so much of what I needed and wanted, so I immediately recognized him. But what a blessing it was to meet someone who showed me what was possible. Ultimately, Jamaal was not "the one," but he reminded me that my true beloved does exist. It is possible for me to have the love I really want. Though short-lived, my time with Jamaal allowed me to experience a happy, healthy, relationship. And for that, I am very grateful.

Another thing I have learned in dating is that you are NEVER wrong to love. It's always a good thing to open yourself to caring deeply for another person, to have the experience of making someone else and their needs a priority. This is truly a divine act, for God is love. So in loving we are participating in divine, heavenly activity and we are better for it. Now loving someone is not necessarily the same as being in a relationship with them. You may love someone you are really not meant to be with; Lord knows I have (!!!), but this does not negate the value of love. So stop beating yourself up over that wretched soul you chose to love. Sure you were exposed to some hurt, and the experience left you with a few scars, and maybe it took you too long to let it go (or maybe you still haven't). This does not make you weak or stupid. It makes you human, courageous and, perhaps, bold. The important part is what choice you make about the relationship if it's not healthy for you. At some point you have to love yourself enough to leave. But the love? It never really ends.

This brings me to my next point: 1 Corinthians 13 is one of my favorite passages about love. I especially resonate with verses 7 and 8. "It [love] always protects, always trusts, always hopes, always perseveres. Love never fails." Growing up in church, I heard that passage at least a million times, but it never meant as much to me until I started dating. I've said on my blog before that any man I've ever loved, I still love. And this is the complete truth. Once you love someone, you're in. You're hooked. For life! The relationship may end but the love never does. When you really love, you never give up on love (not the relationship), the love just keeps on going and going and going.

As for me? I keep dating, keep trying, keep learning, keep dreaming, and keep believing that one day I'll sing along with Etta James, "At laaaaaaaaaast, my looooooove has come aloooooooong..." Oh what a glorious day that will be, but until then I choose to live—live like there's no tomorrow and enjoy my life, work, and experiences in romance. No bitterness. No shame. No regrets. Only faith, hope, and anticipation for the love that is to come. No heartbreak is gonna' stand in my way. Not now. Not ever. Why? Because I chose to heal. And when finally we meet, I will love him—not like I've never been hurt, but I'll love him like I've been healed. Won't you join me?

SPIRITUAL, EMOTIONAL, MENTAL, AND PHYSICAL WELLNESS RESOURCES

Ways To Spend Personal Time With God

"Yet prayer is an invitation to become real, an invitation to shrug off the costumes and masks we wear and to reveal our true faces. The power of prayer, if "power" is the right word, is in its invitation to become unguarded, truthful, and vulnerable before God. "

–Mark Yaconelli[24]

Silent Prayer

This is my absolute favorite type of prayer. It involves nothing but complete silence. Quiet down your world by turning off anything that makes noise. You may decide to dim the lights, up to you. You take as little as 5 minutes (or as much time as you want), and just sit in silence and be with God. You can reflect upon scriptures like "Be still and know that I am God." (Psalm 46:10). Be quiet, restful, and present.

Daily Devotional Reading

24 Yaconelli, Mark. *Downtime: Helping Teenagers Pray.* Grand Rapids: Zondervan, 2008.

This is probably the most widespread kind of devotion. Go to a bookstore and search for inspirational guides and daily devotionals. These usually give you a brief inspirational message, supporting Scripture, and sometimes a short prayer.

Reading Through The Psalms

There are 150 psalms in the Bible written by various people of faith who found themselves in all types of predicaments. Some were in trouble and others were jubilant and happy. Some felt doubtful and abandoned by God, and others felt victorious and celebratory. The broad range of human emotion and experience is covered in the Psalms. Read 1 psalm (chapter in the book of Psalms) a day, or move at whatever pace you like. Then, perhaps quietly reflect for a few moments, and offer a prayer.

Music and prayer

You can always listen to an inspirational, gospel, or other religious song. Sing along with it if you like and then sit quietly and reflect on its meaning. Offer a prayer.

Dance as prayer

I went through a period during my first year of seminary where I felt that I didn't really have the words to say during prayer. Instead I wanted to express with my body what I felt and needed to share with God. So I would literally turn on some inspirational music and dance my prayer to God. This might seem strange but it worked really well for me at the time. I had recently joined the liturgical dance ministry at my school and so I was very in tune with my body and just desired to communicate through movement. These were some of my greatest devotional experiences. I loved it. I believe there is a way that the Spirit understands our "words" of prayer in this kind of expression. I think you can use other creative forms like visual art to pray as well. Try something that works for you.

Engaging Nature

Take a quiet walk. Sit quietly in a park. Lay in the grass. Sit by the beach (lake or pond) and listen to the water. Nature has a way of calming us down and helping us to be quiet. That in turn helps us to be better listeners. Try it. Listen for God's voice. See what happens.

Lectio Divina

"Lectio Divina, literally meaning "divine reading," is an ancient practice of praying the Scriptures. During Lectio Divina, the practitioner listens to the text of the Bible with the "ear of the heart," as if he or she is in conversation with God, and God is suggesting the topics for discussion. The method of Lectio Divina includes moments of reading (lectio), reflecting on (meditatio), responding to (oratio) and resting in (contemplatio) the Word of God with the aim of nourishing and deepening one's relationship with the Divine."[25]

Other Worship and Devotional Resources

Taize'—This is a wonderful community in Taize', France, that has a particular way of employing music and prayer in worship to God; they use words and melodies in a repetitive form, allowing the prayer and singing to naturally build to a climax, and slowly return to a slower pace, achieving a meditative experience. Their unique music and worship practices are used in churches throughout the world. You might explore churches in your local area who occasionally offer Taize' worship experiences. I always find Taize' resources to be incredibly powerful! Visit www.taize.fr to learn more.

These are just a few ideas, but there are many, many more ways of praying, meditating, and spending time with God. I believe this is vital to our healing and complete restoration. So no matter how you do it, just be sure to get it done. And be honest and real in your time with God.

Books for Finding Quiet and Nurturing Your Relationship with God

Enjoy The Silence: A 30 Day Experiment In Listening To God *by Maggie and Duffy Robbins.*[26] This is

---

25 www.contemplativeoutreach.org, 8/24/14

26 Robbins, Maggie and Robbins, Duffy. *Enjoy The Silence: A 30 Day Experiment In Listening To God.* Grand Rapids:

a wonderful book that will lead you in 30 days of quiet reflection and mediation on the scriptures. It translates the ancient practice of lectio divina (see defined above) into a very meaningful daily devotional experience for the modern day person. Though this book was developed with youth in mind, I believe it can be a powerfully transformative tool for anyone! It certainly was for me.

Having A Mary Heart In A Martha World: Finding Intimacy With God in the Busyness of Life by Joanna Weaver.[27] Joanna Weaver is one of my favorite authors ever and I will always appreciate the labor of love that is this book. In her writing she beautifully captures the character of Mary, sister of Martha and Lazarus in the gospels, and how she unapologetically blocked out the busyness of the world around her in exchange for a much needed quiet moment of restoration with Jesus. If you are feeling the need for such a renewal, then please take a walk with Joanna into the world of Mary and Martha and find your peace!

Downtime: Helping Teenagers Pray by Mark Yaconelli.[28] Downtime. Don't we all need it? Sometimes

---

Zondervan, 2005.

27 Weaver, Joanna. *Having A Mary Heart In A Martha World: Finding Intimacy With God in the Busyness of Life.* Colorado Springs: WaterBrook Press, 2000.

28 Yaconelli, Mark. *Downtime: Helping Teenagers Pray.* Grand

we need to get a way from the craziness of life and make time for prayer. Though this book is targeted to teenagers, I believe it has powerful insight to help anyone looking to develop a prayer life. I've definitely used it for both myself and my work in ministry with young people.

Jesus Calling: **Enjoying Peace in His Presence** by Sarah Young[29] This is another really awesome resource for developing a spiritual discipline of spending time with God. This is a year-long devotional that provides a brief devotional message and supportive Scriptures to guide your quiet time each day.

Noise from the Nooma Series by Rob Bell.[30] I LOVE this resource! Noise is a 10 minute filmthat shows us the importance of clearing our headspace, and finding solace in prayer. Our world is amazingly noisy. Here Rob Bell guides us into a place of quiet and calm where we can meet God and be restored. [31]

Rapids: Zondervan, 2008.

29 Young, Sarah. *Jesus Calling: Enjoying Peace in His Presence.* Nashville: Thomas Nelson, 2004.

30 Bell, Rob. *Nooma: Noise.* DVD. Grand Rapids: Zondervan, 2005.

31 Available on DVD or for electronic download at nooma.org

Helpful Scriptures on Silence, Meditation, and Prayer

Search your hearts and be silent.
Psalm 4:4

Be still and know that I am God.
Psalm 46:10

But Jesus often withdrew to lonely places and prayed.
Luke 5:16

Then Jesus said, "Come to me, all of you who are weary and carry heavy burdens, and I will give you rest."
Matthew 11:28

Then from the cloud came a voice that said, "This is my Son, my Chosen; listen to him!"
Luke 9:35

And there he went into a cave, and spent the night in that place; and behold, the word of the Lord came to him, and He said to him, "What are you doing here, Elijah?" So he said, "I have been very zealous for the Lord God of hosts; for the children of Israel have forsaken Your covenant, torn down Your altars, and killed Your prophets with the sword. I alone am left; and they seek to take my

life." Then He said, "Go out, and stand on the mountain before the Lord." And behold, the Lord passed by, and a great and strong wind tore into the mountains and broke the rocks in pieces before the Lord, but the Lord was not in the wind; and after the wind an earthquake, but the Lord was not in the earthquake; and after the earthquake a fire, but the Lord was not in the fire; and after the fire a still small voice.
1 Kings 19:9-12 (New King James Version)

I'm asking God for one thing, only one thing: To live with him in his house my whole life long. I'll contemplate his beauty; I'll study at his feet. That's the only quiet, secure place in a noisy world. The perfect getaway, far from the buzz of traffic.
Psalm 27:4-5 (The Message)

Now as they went on their way, he entered a certain village, where a woman named Martha welcomed him into her home. She had a sister named Mary, who sat at the Lord's feet and listened to what he was saying. But Martha was distracted by her many tasks; so she came to him and asked, "Lord, do you not care that my sister has left me to do all the work by myself? Tell her then to help me." But the Lord answered her, "Martha, Martha, you are worried and distracted by many things; there is need of only one thing. Mary has chosen the better part, which will not be taken away from her.
Luke 10:38-42

Don't worry about anything, but in everything by prayer and supplication with thanksgiving let your requests be made known to God. And the peace of God, which surpasses all understanding, will guard your hearts and your minds in Christ Jesus. Finally, beloved, whatever is true, whatever is honorable, whatever is just, whatever is pure, whatever is pleasing, whatever is commendable, if there is any excellence and if there is anything worthy of praise, think about these things.
Philippians 4:6-8

MY EXPERIENCE WITH SPIRITUAL DIRECTION

Spiritual Direction is Sacred Space

Spiritual direction is something I highly recommend. I have been seeing my spiritual director, Diana, for about 3 ½ years now. She is awesome! What I love most about our time together is that Diana really helps me to see the love and grace of God active in my life. While it may seem obvious when God is extending mercy, direction, or love, I have found that I am often unaware of all God's amazing activity happening all around me.

When I come to Diana to share a problem, she always helps me to reframe it and directs me to explore how God is equipping me in the midst of it. Even in the darkest of places, I am led to take notice of God's mercy and love pouring out where I had not noticed it. It's so easy to miss it; believe me. Spiritual directors help bring you to an awareness of Divine activity in your life.

Spiritual Direction is Safe Space

I can tell Diana, any- and everything without fear of judgment. Your spiritual director is not trying to show you how wrong you are. Rather they help you navigate the tough terrain of life, learning its lessons, fostering spiritual growth, making you more attuned to the voice and move of God along the way. They are holy companions, journeying with you as you go.

Spiritual Direction as Spiritual Discipline

Much of what happens in spiritual direction occurs outside of meeting times. Diana often gives me homework and exercises to do in between sessions that help me develop my spiritual discipline. Whether it's quiet time, a journal exercise, or whatever. Spiritual direction is often called directed prayer, though it may or may not be prayer in the traditional sense (getting on your knees and clasping your hands together.) The methods of spiritual direction are varied, sometimes traditional and other times more innovative. They should always be tailored to fit you, leading you to be attentive to the presence and love of God in your life. And that makes all the difference in your perspective, decision-making, and state of mind and spirit.

Spiritual Direction as Spiritual Renewal

Seeing my spiritual director is always an incredible lift

in my spirit. Most of the time, I leave there feeling on top of the world. It really is time spent in God's presence. And just that presence, transforms my reality and strengthens and inspires me for the days ahead.

SPIRITUAL DIRECTION, HEARTBREAK, AND HEALING:
AN INTERVIEW WITH MY SPIRITUAL DIRECTOR, DIANA

How would you define spiritual direction?
Spiritual Direction is a meeting between a Spiritual Director, aka, a trained listener, and a person who is seeking more in their life. It is an opportunity to share one's story and gain God's perspective on one's journey.

How do you approach spiritual direction with your clients? What's your philosophy of spiritual direction?
My prayer before each spiritual direction session includes, "Please keep me out of Your way, dear God!" There is always a Third party present during a spiritual direction session. As a director I am listening to our ultimate Director and to the person (directee) who is sharing their story.

What kind of training/certification did you go through to become a spiritual director?
My Spiritual Direction certificate is from the Center for Spirituality and Lay Ministry, Sacred Heart University located in Fairfield, CT. During the four-year course I

submitted sixteen book reflections, one hundred-twenty reflections on published articles, twenty-four verbatims on spiritual direction sessions, participated in peer supervision among other Spiritual Directors, met with a supervisor thirty-two times, attended four silent retreats, had sessions with directees and submitted eight self-evaluation papers. Each year there was one week of intensive classes to attend in order to become certified.

How has going to see a spiritual director been helpful in your own life?

For me, being heard and the depth of my experience validated, was life changing. After 23 three years of being in spiritual direction, I continue to discover who I was created to be. As I continue to share my story as it is unfolding, my relationship with my Creator God grows because I see God's Hand in all that I experience.

How can spiritual direction be helpful to someone seeking healing from heartbreak?

"What people need is a good listening to!" These words were given to me on a greeting card. When a person who is heartbroken shares their pain in a non-partial, confidential venue, the potential is there to restore their inner peace and regain their boldness to be the person they were created to be.

What would you say are the most important factors to consider when selecting a spiritual

director?

Very often a director and directee do not know each other prior to the first spiritual direction session. General expectations should be shared by both parties with the understanding that each can cancel the arrangement at any time. Eventually a trust should develop between the director and directee, the directee's sharing should become easier and an appetite for discovery should be enhanced.

Is there any other information you'd like to share with my readers about spiritual direction?

We hear and read more about physical and mental health than we do about spiritual health. Our bodies and minds require nutrition and exercise. What nourishes our soul and our inner self where our Creator resides? Spiritual direction allows one to safely speak about what is going on in their life, explore what to do or where to go next and seek God's perspective on all of it. When our heart's desires and God's loving intentions for us come together, it is a time of celebration!

Visit www.sdiworld.org to find a spiritual director in your area, or to learn more.

RESOURCES FOR MENTAL WELLNESS

I know that in reading this book it is possible that some really painful moments from your past (or present) may have risen to the surface for you. I am not sure what the experience has been like, but if you are feeling overwhelmed and think you could benefit from talking to a professional counselor, therapist, or other mental health professional, please do take action. I have provided minimal resource information below for you in case you need guidance in reaching out for support. ***The information provided here is no replacement for actual medical care. Always contact your doctor (primary care physician) first*** *if you believe you need mental wellness support and or treatment. Take your health seriously. You are worth it. Don't have health insurance? Visit www.healthcare.gov. You may also contact your local city or county health department to find local resources available to you.*

WEBSITES

National Alliance on Mental Health
www.nami.org

American Psychological Association
www.apa.org

American Psychiatric Association
www.psych.org

American Association for Marriage and Family Therapy
www.aamft.org

BOOKS

Not Alone: Reflections on Faith and Depression—A 40-Day Devotional by Monica A. Coleman, www.monicaacoleman.com. Dr. Monica A. Coleman, is an accomplished writer, activist, and scholar. In this devotional, she draws from her own experience and provides much needed encouragement and inspiration for those struggling with depression.[32]

Black Pain: It Just Looks Like We're Not Hurting by Terrie M. Williams. This is a really comprehensive text that explores mental health issues, with particular focus on the Black community. Very insightful work.[33]

CREATIVE ARTS THERAPIES AND HEALING

I was absolutely amazed when I did research on the various creative arts therapies and learned about their potential to aid in healing for someone experiencing emotional pain. If traditional types of therapies aren't something you want to try, consider music, art, drama, dance, poetry, or other types of creative arts or

32 Coleman, Monica A. *Not Alone: Reflections on Faith and Depression—A 40-Day Devotional.* Monica Coleman, 2012.

33 Williams, Terrie. *Black Pain: It Just Looks Like We're Not Hurting.* New York: Scribner A Division of Simon and Schuster, 2008.

expressive therapies. Or use them in concert with more classical approaches to therapy. Below I have given some definitions from various professional creative arts organizations. I also have to interviews that follow with an expressive therapist and an art therapist.

Please Note** **In all minimal research I did in creative arts therapies, none of these approaches require that a client be proficient in the art itself in order for therapy to be affective.** In other words, you need not be able to paint well or draw to benefit from art therapy, or to sing well or play an instrument for music therapy to be helpful to you. The point is to use the art to assess and process what you are feeling, and to provide intervention. So don't let your perceived amateur skill stop you from trying it!

National Coalition For Creative Arts Therapies Association

www.nccata.org

"Creative Arts Therapists are human service professionals who use arts modalities [music, art, dance, poetry, drama] and creative processes for the purpose of ameliorating disability and illness and optimizing health and wellness...There are more than 15,000 Creative Arts Therapists practicing in the United States and around the world. Creative Arts Therapy organizations have been active in this country for over 50 years." [34]

---

34 "About NCCATA," National Coalition For Creative Arts

American Music Therapy Association (AMTA)

www.musictherapy.org

"Music Therapy is an established health profession in which music is used within a therapeutic relationship to address physical, emotional, cognitive, and social needs of individuals." [35]

Art Therapy—American Art Therapy Association (AATA)

www.arttherapy.org

"Art therapy is a mental health profession in which clients, facilitated by the art therapist, use art media, the creative process, and the resulting artwork to explore their feelings, reconcile emotional conflicts, foster self-awareness, manage behavior and addictions, develop social skills, improve reality orientation, reduce anxiety, and increase self-esteem." [36]

American Dance Therapy Association (ADTA)

www.adta.org

"Based on the empirically supported premise that the body, mind and spirit are interconnected, the American

---

Therapies Association accessed September 2, 2014, http://www.nccata.org/#!aboutnccata/czsv.

35 "Definitions and Quotes About Music Therapy," American Music therapy Association, accessed September 2, 2014, http://www.musictherapy.org/about/quotes.

36 "About Art Therapy," American Art Therapy Association, accessed September 2, 2014, http://www.artherapy.org.

Dance Therapy Association defines dance/movement therapy as the psychotherapeutic use of movement to further the emotional, cognitive, physical and social integration of the individual."–ADTA Dance therapy is used with people of all ages, races and ethnic backgrounds in individual, couples, family and group therapy formats. Therapists use dance and body movement to assess and treat persons needing development." [37]

North American Drama Therapy Association
www.nadta.org
"Drama Therapy is an active, experiential approach to facilitating change. Through storytelling, projective play, purposeful improvisation, and performance, participants are invited to rehearse desired behaviors, practice being in relationship, expand and find flexibility between life roles, and perform the change they wish to be and see in the world." [38]

National Association for Poetry Therapists
www.poetrytherapy.org
"For the past 30 years, NAPT members have forged a community of healers and lovers of words and language.

---

37 "About Dance/Movement Therapy," American Dance Therapy Association, accessed September 2, 2014, http://www.adta.org/About_DMT

38 "What Is Drama Therapy?" North American Drama Therapy Association, accessed September 2, 2014, www.nadta.org

We are psychotherapists, counselors, psychologists, social workers, and psychiatrists. We are poets, journal keepers, storytellers, and songwriters. We are teachers, librarians, adult educators, and university professors. We are doctors, nurses, occupational/ recreational therapists; ministers, pastoral counselors, and spiritual directors. We are artists, dancers, dramatists, musicians, and writers. We work in many settings where people deal with personal and communal pain and the search for growth. As poetry therapists, we use all forms of literature and the language arts, and we are united by our love of words, and our passion for enhancing the lives of others and ourselves." [39]

EXPRESSIVE THERAPY, HEARTBREAK, AND HEALING EXCERPT OF MY INTERVIEW WITH EXPRESSIVE THERAPIST DAWN MCKINLEY

How would you describe the therapy you practice?
I am an expressive therapist, specializing in music therapy. My master's degree is in expressive therapy and mental health counseling. I am not board-certified as a music therapist but am a licensed professional counselor in the state of Connecticut.

---

39 "About The National Association For Poetry Therapy," National Association For Poetry Therapy, accessed September 2, 2014, www.poetrytherapy.org

Expressive therapy is a combination of all of the arts. I went to Leslie University in Cambridge, MA.[40] So you have to take a battery of arts classes. You have to take music, dance, drama. You have to learn how to do what are called intermodal transfers from one modality to another. So for instance, I learned that as an expressive therapist, you would transfer [do intermodal transfers] with someone who has depression. For example, sometimes people who are depressed generally may have a walk that is slow, their bodies are hunched over, their faces look sad. And what you can miss in other types of therapy is the opportunity for the patient to really understand their bodies and help themselves to make those transitions to feel better. We can start with just simple movement, putting on music that is uplifting. For instance, the second you hear "I'm Every Woman," you get really happy, your body starts moving. Then we would process. "What was it like to have your body move straight up? What was it like to move within that? Then I might do a transfer to art. "If you were to give it a color what does it look like?" Then play the song again. Then [have the patient] take a paintbrush and paint the movement. "What does that [the movement] look like?" That's an example of an intermodal transfer from one modality (of art) to another.

Along with all the music, art, movement, and drama, I

40 Dawn shared later in the interview that Leslie University is widely considered the home of expressive therapy.

also had a whole battery of psych classes: assessment, career development, psych 101, all of that. So that's what an expressive therapist does. You have to know all of those modalities.

How would expressive therapy be helpful to a person experiencing emotional pain, more specifically going through a heartbreak?

The thing about the heartbreak, you're right, it's emotional pain. And music therapy is particularly great for the healing of that heartbreak.

A lot of times people go through depression. A lot of times they'll go through some apprehension about going on to new relationships. They have difficulty sometimes with social interactions because "I'm lonely. I've lost someone. Nobody wants me," those types of feelings and emotions. And anger. "I'm just mad at every man in the entire world, or every woman. I'm mad at the world. I'm mad at God, just angry all the time because my heart is broken.

Well, the interventions with music therapy are just sweet! The brain and your body reacts completely to music. Whether it is our emotions, it physiologically changes and transforms your body to the emotional pain.

I would use a number of interventions to assess what's going on, do an intervention to assess what's going on through music listening. So talk to me about "How does the music affect you? When you are listing to this music what kind of feelings come up for you? What kind of emotions? And it's intentioned. So for instance, if I am looking to find a way t to help them express their anger, I might play Whitney Houston's Where Do Broken Hearts Go? I might do an Alanis Morissette song where she was angry about her boyfriend getting a new girlfriend.[41]

And then we would analyze the lyrics.

We'd do some listening. We'd do some analyzing. And then we'd do some talking, the processing piece. Talk to me about those deep dark feelings. A lot of times it's hard to express those feelings. It's hard to put a name to it. So music gives you the opportunity to say what you can't really verbally say. That would be one of things I would do.

If you're talking about it in terms of a treatment plan is concerned, what are some of the treatment tools in a clinical sense? I would also ask them "what music do you like right now?" Have them bring in some music. Have them learn how to play a particular song that they like.

Or better yet, sometimes even do some drumming.

---

41 Alanis Morisette, "You Outta Know" by Alanis Morisette and Glen Ballard, recorded in 1994 and 1995 at Westlake Recording Studios on *Jagged Little Pill*, Maverick, Reprise.

Drumming regulates your heartbeat. Drumming is also relaxation. You'd think that it's going to be extremely agitating, but it really isn't. It depends on your rhythm and it depends our interaction with the patient. So my relationship is really important with the patient. So I can say follow this rhythm, or I could ask them, "create a rhythm on how you're feeling right now." And then talk about what was it like to *hear* those emotions and those feelings played out on the drum? What was that like?

Or I've done, many times, songwriting. It's basically poetry. There's no proficiency (required). You don't have to be a virtuoso. But, "What do you want to say? How do you want to address some of those issues? How do you want to express the anger? How do you want to address the loneliness? How do you want to address the fact that it's over? And how do you move on? What do you see in the future? Create a song that may be helpful in helping you to say I *can* move on. I *do* have goals. I *do* have a future. And singing it. You've been in your car and your jam comes on and your whole body and thought changes. You start thinking positive as opposed to negative.

Dawn McKinley, MA, LPC- Owner
Licensed Professional Counselor
http://www.dtmcounselingservices.com

ART THERAPY, HEARTBREAK, AND HEALING
AN INTERVIEW WITH ART THERAPIST MARTINA MARTIN

What is art therapy? How would you describe the therapy you practice?

Art Therapy is a mental health profession that utilizes the process of art making to help individuals process things they can't find words for, while seeking to improve and enhance their physical, mental and emotional well-being. My experience has focused on individual and group art therapy for children and adults of all ages. Some of my specialties include trauma, mood disorders, HIV, LGBT concerns, chronic mental illness, chronic health conditions, multicultural issues, spirituality and existential concerns, substance abuse and addiction, as well as grief and loss. My theoretical orientation for art therapy is eclectic and combines person-centered, relational, existential and cognitive theories with the practical application of skill building in the areas of mindfulness, emotional awareness and regulation, as well as interpersonal effectiveness.

Could art therapy be helpful to a person experiencing emotional pain?

Absolutely! The need to create and engage in the expressive arts is a universal trait of humanity that has been in existence since the beginning of time. From the 40,000 year old sculptures and paintings of the prehistoric era, to the modern day "tags" of urban graffiti artists, human beings have consistently relied upon marks, images and sculptures to communicate, transform, heal and inspire. Research has shown that when an individual is engaged in a creative process, such as art therapy, they can expect an increase in serotonin levels in the brain, which can lessen emotional stress and anxiety and ultimately elevate their mood.

Do you think art therapy would be helpful to a person struggling through a tough heartbreak? If so, how?

Absolutely! When a person experiences a significant loss, like a bad break up, it is not uncommon for words to fail and be deemed insufficient. In those dark moments of the soul, catharsis is what's needed, and art therapy provides a perfect platform to express one's raw and felt emotions in an uninhibited and non-judgmental way.

How might you approach an art therapy session with a person needing healing from a devastating break-up?

The first thing I would do when working with a client who has just gone through a tough break up is to encourage them to create an "I Feel" mandala. A mandala is a Sanskrit word that refers to a circular form, which in this instance, would be lightly drawn in pencil on a piece of white paper. Using the materials provided, including oil or chalk pastels, I would encourage the client to complete the sentence, "I Feel...." There is no right or wrong, and no good or bad in this type of exercise. The circular form may be used, or ignored; the purpose is to simply allow the client to own, acknowledge and track their feelings in the moment. Clients may be encouraged to jot down any words or thoughts that come to mind and to sign and date their artwork. Creating a daily "I Feel" mandala is a great way to track one's emotions, and much like a journal, when veiwed over a period of time, it can give the client a tremendous amount of insight into the ways in which their thoughts, feelings and emotions have fluctuated. Studies have shown that drawing within a circular form can instill a sense of calm within the artist and creating mandalas have been linked to a reduction in blood pressure!

Is there anything else you'd like to share about the connection between art therapy and heartbreak/ emotional wellness?

When used within the context of a professional therapy relationship, art therapy can facilitate artistic self-expression and aid those who are recovering from heartbreak. Whether an individual needs to explore their feelings, reconcile an emotional conflict, gain self-awareness, improve their social skills or increase their self esteem, art therapy can help them improve or restore their sense of well-being.

Martina E. Martin, M.Div., M.A., ATR-BC, LPC
Counselor/Art Therapist/Fine Artist/Workshop Facilitator
www.martinamartin.com

GET EDUCATED ABOUT SEXUALLY TRANSMITTED DISEASES

I wrote very candidly in this book about my personal experience with STDs. I chose to share that because I wanted to encourage anyone going through something similar. There are a lot of stigmas around this topic and often people don't care to talk about it openly, particularly in faith communities. If you have been diagnosed with an STD, know that God loves you no matter what your diagnosis. Anyone that tells you differently is LYING!!! Your life is not over. Again, whoever says it is, is a LIAR! I say...Go after your healing—physical, emotional, and spiritual. They are yours to have. Reach out for the resources of healing, support, and love available to you! I've listed a few of my favorite resources below!
—Ari

FOR TESTING AND TREATMENT...

Planned Parenthood
Planned Parenthood is probably the largest and most trusted provider of healthcare specializing in sexual and reproductive health. They educate communities and provide a vast array of **diagnostic, preventive,** and **treatment** services for people diagnosed with **various sexually transmitted diseases**. If you have reason to believe you are at risk for any STD, **PLEASE GET**

TESTED. Find your local Planned Parenthood at www.plannedparenthood.org.

For Research and Education...
The Centers For Disease Control (CDC)

CDC continues to do meaningful work through its research and education initiatives to help us better understand and treat disease. **To learn more about a particular sexual transmitted disease**, prevention, and treatment visit at www.cdc.gov/std.

FOR AWARENESS AND EDUCATION...

Red Pump Project

I love this organization! Their "mission is **to promote HIV prevention** through **education**, and open dialogue about the issues that surround sexual and reproductive health." What I love is that they utilize very innovative, creative, and relevant methods like blogging (amongst others) to educate everyone! Learn more about their work and how you can get involved at www.theredpumpproject.com

FOR CHURCH INVOLVEMENT AND SERVICE...

The Balm In Gilead, Inc.

The Balm In Gilead "develops educational and training programs specifically designed to meet the unique needs of African American and African congregations that strive to become community centers for healing, education, and disease prevention." One of their signature and most powerful programs is the National Week of Prayer for the Healing of AIDS, which "brings national attention to the AIDS epidemic in the United States and the extraordinary role faith communities can and are playing in AIDS prevention, education, service, and advocacy." Think your church should get involved? Visit www.balmingilead.org and www.nationalweekofprayerforthehealingofaids.org.

The Naked Truth: Young, Beautiful, and HIV Positive by Marvelyn Brown
When I read this book several years ago, I was so moved by Marvelyn's story. (So moved in fact, that I took my church youth group to hear her speak here in Kansas City once. It was really a great presentation, both engaging and enlightening). In her compelling autobiography, Marvelyn shares her experience of being diagnosed with HIV at the age of 19. She draws attention to critical social issues surrounding HIV and promotes prevention and education. It's an honest, well-written, and powerful story. Check it out. Visit Marvelyn online at www.marvelynbrown.com.

Other helpful online resources:
www.aids.gov
http://www.nlm.nih.gov/medlineplus/sexuallytransmitteddiseases.html

A few final thoughts...

Please note that the **information provided here is NOT a replacement** for seeking **good medical care**. **Go see your doctor if you need to be tested for an STD or if you have concerns about your sexual and reproductive health.**

If you don't have medical insurance, check out www.healthcare.gov to see how you can get medical coverage. Reach out to your local health department to get information on resources in your city/town for prevention, testing, and treatment of STDs. You can find contact information for your local health department by going to your city or county government's website or by looking in the local phone book.

Early detection and treatment of STDs is helpful to you. Don't delay!!! You are worth it.

Me rocking my Red Pump Project Gear!!!

RELATIONSHIP READINESS INTERVIEW

Part of the healing process is preparing yourself for love the next time it comes around. This means taking inventory of your own mental, emotional, and spiritual state before starting a new relationship, as well as assessing your own fears, desires, inhibitions, and expectations. This list is certainly not meant to be exhaustive; feel free to edit it as needed. However, these are the questions I've learned I need to ask any potential partner and myself before beginning a relationship. You don't have to approach this like homework; it can be as casual as you like. You don't even have to do this in one sitting. Just be sure to have the critical conversations necessary before starting a new love adventure! Make sure you and your partner are ready! Set your relationship up for success.

INSTRUCTIONS

Answer each question honestly. Give the questions to your partner to do the same.
Discuss your answers with your potential partner.
If you don't know an answer, that's okay. Take note of that.
Don't rush it, but do continue to ponder the question.
If any of the answers that you or your partner provides give you pause, don't ignore it. Honor that hesitation.
Choose wisely for yourself.

QUESTIONS TO ASK YOURSELF

What I Want

Why do I want a relationship?

What long-term outcomes am I seeking? Marriage, long-term commitment, friendship, casual dating, a good time, etc.

How much of my time and energy am I willing to give to this relationship?

Am I willing to put forth the effort of being in a relationship?

What do I think are characteristics of a healthy relationship?

What are my top 3 most important factors in a relationship?

What are my primary and secondary love languages?**

What I Feel

Am I over my ex? Have I really healed from my last heartbreak?

Am I emotionally available? Will I open up to this person?

How have my experiences in past relationships changed (for better or worse) the way I feel about and approach relationships now? What are my scars?

What are my insecurities? Are they heightened when I'm dating someone? How, so?

Do you have any hesitation about starting a relationship? If so, describe it in detail.

Do you have any fears about starting a relationship? If so, describe it in detail.

Is now a good time for me to be in a relationship, mentally, emotionally, and spiritually?

What I Feel For Them

Do I really like this person? Not what they do, or even how they treat me but do I honestly like them as a person?

What do I like about them?

What do I not like about them?

Do I know enough about my partner to begin an intimate relationship?

What I Want From Them

What do I expect of my partner?

What am I looking for in a partner, and does this potential partner have those qualities?

What things will I absolutely not tolerate from my partner?

Do I actually want a relationship with *this* person?

Do I have any hesitation about starting a relationship with this person? If so, describe.

Do I have any fears about starting a relationship with this person? What are they?

At what pace do I think things should progress?

Are there any marks of success I want to see?

QUESTIONS TO ASK YOUR POTENTIAL PARTNER

What You Want

What is your long-term goal for this relationship? Marriage, long-term commitment, friendship, a good time, etc.

What do you think are the characteristics of a healthy relationship?

Do you have any deal-breakers? If so, what are they?

What are your top three most important factors in a relationship?

What are your primary and secondary love languages?

How You Feel

Are you over your ex? Have you really healed the pain of your last heartbreak?

Are you emotionally available to me?

How have your experiences in past relationships improved or damaged the way you approach and feel about relationships now? What are your scars?

What are your insecurities?

Do you have any hesitation about starting a relationship? If so, describe it in detail.

Do you have any fears about starting a relationship? If so, describe it in detail.

Is now a good time for you to start a relationship? Are you in a good place emotionally, mentally, and spiritually?

What You Feel For Me

Why do you want to be with me?

What do you like about me?

What do you not like about me?

Do you feel you know enough about me to pursue a more intimate relationship with me?

What Do You Want From Me

What do you expect of me as your partner?

What are your non-negotiables? In other words, what must you have in your relationship?

What things (if any) will you absolutely not tolerate from me?

Do you have any fears about entering into a relationship *with me*? What are they?

Do you have any hesitation about entering into a relationship *with me*? Describe it in detail.

At what pace do you think things should progress?

Are there any marks of success you want to see?

HELPFUL RESOURCE!!!

** A love language is a concept developed by **Dr. Gary Chapman** and presented in his famous work, ***The Five Love Languages: The Secret To Love That Lasts***[42] It explores five primary ways of expressing love: words of affirmation, physical touch, acts of service, receiving gifts, and quality time. I highly recommend anyone seeking love and relationship (of any kind) to read this book! It is a very insightful resource for understanding

42 Chapman, Gary. *The Five Love Languages: The Secret To Love That Lasts.* Northfield Publishing: Chicago, 2010.

yourself better and *how you love.* I highly recommend you visit the website to take your quiz (free!) to find out your love language. It is definitely good to know this about yourself and for your potential partner to know his (or hers) also so that you are both in a better position to understand one another's words, actions and expression of love. Visit www.5lovelanguages.com to take your assessment.

HOW TO REFLECT AND MOVE ON!

Much of what I have shared in this book came to me during times of reflection post-break up. Taking the time to really reflect upon what happened in my relationship, what caused the heartbreak, why I made the choices that I did was vital to my moving forward in life. So I encourage you to do that too. This is a prime opportunity for learning more about ourselves, and about love and life. We do ourselves, our families, and our future lovers a great service when we choose to think honestly and soberly about our past pain. In the days after a crushing heartbreak we can grow by leaps and bounds into a better, wiser, stronger version of ourselves. So I've included a few reflection questions to guide you as you reflect, should you choose to do this exercise.

Here are the rules of engagement.

Ask God to help you. Pray for clarity and growth in the reflection process.

Be honest with yourself. Don't rewrite history. Look at the circumstances for what they really were and how things really happened.

Take responsibility for your stuff. If it's yours, then own it. Do not shame yourself for your choices. If you feel embarrassed a bit by something you did, that's normal, but don't beat up on yourself. Examine closely your choices and behavior, but be gentle with yourself.

Let the lessons emerge organically. Don't force it. If there's something you don't understand yet, sit with it for a while. Use your resources: family, friends, who have a mature perspective. (Speaking to someone older might really be helpful.) Again you don't have to divulge everything to the world, but discernment happens best in the context of community. Be selective, but do seek out a different perspective.

Keep an open heart and mind throughout this process.

Don't allow preconceived ideas and raw feelings block your learning.

When the lessons emerge, acknowledge them.

Be willing to change and put them into action.

Pray some more.

Good questions to ask

What were the positive things I experienced in this relationship?

What negative moments did I experience in this relationship?

What things went right? How did I contribute?

What went wrong? How did I contribute?

What was the core of my pain in this relationship? How did I contribute or respond?

What was the core of my partner's pain? How did I contribute or respond?

What fruitful choices did I make in this relationship? How did I come to choose that?

What were some of the less than fruitful choices I made? Why did I choose that? What would have been a better choice?

What moments and experiences in this relationship can I be grateful for?

What areas did I improve upon in comparison to my last relationship?

What positive outcomes can I take with me from this experience (lessons, new practices, insights)?

What did I learn about what I like and don't like?

ACKNOWLEDGEMENTS

This is a dream come true. I remember telling a panel of distinguished PhD-holding Howard University professors that I had plans of one day writing books. This was during an interview as part of the application process for entry into the Ronald E. McNair Post-Baccalaureate Achievement Program when I was just a sophomore at dear old Howard. I was 19. I had no idea how I would do this or what kind of book I would write. And amazingly, after all kinds of experiences, academic pursuits, and life's adventures and misadventures, here I am having done it! Praise be to Almighty God! I've done it!

But not without the help of so many...

So let me first thank every one of my teachers at any school I've ever attended for any subject. Thank you for teaching me to read, write, think critically, and learn. I am here because of you. Truly.

Special thanks to all my teachers at Garrett-Evangelical Theological Seminary for teaching me how to think theologically, and opening my mind and heart and giving me new tools to critically engage and examine our faith.

Thank you to every person that has helped with this project. To my Grandma Freida, thank you sooo much for proofreading my first draft (for free!) LOL! To my editor, Katara, thanks for helping transform the manuscript into something really beautiful and polished. Thanks for all your advice and support along the way. Thank you to Jodi for studying my work carefully, listening, and creating a cover and overall design that perfectly interprets my story and resonates with my readers. Thank you Tiphani and Azarel for teaching me sooooo much about publishing, and for doing it from the heart. Thanks for long phone calls, sharing resources, and giving of yourselves so generously to ensure my success! Thanks to all my TBSP (The Best Sellers Project) cohorts and fellow alum for your encouragement, feedback, and support! Thank you Queenie for choosing me for Radiant YOUniversity and pushing me past my fears towards my ultimate purpose and passion. Thank you for coaching that changed my life and gave me clarity I'd never had! To Lauren, thank you sis, for creating a beautiful website that perfectly captured my vision. And thank you Stacey for guiding me through my first ever photo shoot and producing those fabulous shots! Thanks you Chris Truss and Mechelle for making me beautiful for the shoot! Thank you Dawn McKinley, Martina Martin, and Diana Mitchell for so generously sharing your work with my readers. You are all AMAZING!!!

To my Ms. Rachelle, for being an inspiration and leading the way as an author. To my sis Tanesha for always giving your perspective on things as a fellow author, and for being there for me every step of the way!!!

To Shanel and Aunt Shannon, for being unofficial members of all my "committees!" LOL! Thank you for advice, Starbucks meetings, and early strategy sessions! Bless you both!!!

Thank you Joey for your unwavering support of me, and for selflessly pushing me to stand in my truth, for wanting me to shine! To Jamaal for showing me that real love is possible. To Candy and Shaine, thank you for being there and for all your encouragement! Thank you to Jason, Danielle, and Jennifer for listening to my ideas day after day and sharing your feedback as I thought through this work. To Soror Bourgie (lol), thanks for sharing resources, love and support! To Michele and Jon, for calls, cheerleading, and constant encouragement during the writing process. To all my GEBS fam for all your support! To my very much good best friend Soror Candice (inside joke), for reminding me why I started in the first place and showing me how to finish when it got hard, thank you! And thank you Candice, Micki, Tiffani, Dominique, Holly, and Diana for living through these experiences of heartbreak with me, lending me shoulders to cry on and space to heal. Thanks to my friends, Sheriece, Kristen, Alexis, Angela, Alexis, Ashley, Natalie, Kim, Shannon, Jenna, and Pope for your love and support!

To April, Allison, Darlene, and Mishawn thanks a billion for your valuable feedback, loyalty and LOVE! Y'all are EVERYTHING!!!

Thank you Rev. Kathy Brown, Bishop and Mrs. Starnes, Presiding Elder Moulton, and the Missouri

Conference for your incredible support and encouragement. Thank you my Pastor, Rev. Michael Murray and my entire church family for your support and love! Thank you Metropolitan for spending so many years teaching me about faith.

To the entire Moss and Williams families and all other extended family for EVERYTHING!!! Thanks for teaching me the love of God and for always loving me for me. A special shout out to my Auntie Kim, my ride or die, for a billion Facebook posts and so much encouragement!!! LOL!!! Thank you Aunt Janet for your constant checking in and prayers. Thanks Cousin Lisa for your invaluable tax and business advice! To my Cousin Danny, thank you for blazing a trail for me and for building such an incredible legacy! Love you!

Thanks to my Godparents for always being super supportive, and always providing a place for me to retreat from the rest of the world. I wrote the first words of this book in your home on Thanksgiving Day 2012.
To Daddy and Tanya, for always lending your support before I even ask. Thank you Mama for being my #1 Cheerleader! To Mom and Dad thanks so much for sharing your story so openly with my readers!!!

Thank you to every person who ever asked me, "When's the book coming out?" or "How's the writing going?" THANK YOU for holding me accountable and pushing me to actually FINISH!

With love, —Ari